Spotlight

on
Early Childhood
Music Education

Spotlight
on
Early Childhood
Music Education

MENC MENC
MENC MENC
MENC MENC
The National Association for Music Education

MENC would like to thank the MEA state editors throughout the country,
who facilitate the distribution
of essential information to MENC members in their states.

Contents

Section 3 Assessment

The Spotlight series comprises articles that have appeared in magazines of MENC state affiliates over the past several years. The purpose of the series is to broaden the audience for the valuable work that is being done by music educators across the country. Were it not for the dedication of the state editors and article authors, this series would not be possible. MENC would like to thank these individuals for their contributions and to encourage others to share their expertise through MEA and MENC publications.

Introduction

Music experiences that take place during the early childhood years are important for a number of reasons. They support expressive, emotional, intellectual, social, and creative growth in young children, and they create a foundation upon which future music learning is built. While young learners benefit from music experiences in many different contexts, it is important to expose children to music in a developmentally appropriate way. In many situations, early childhood music educators work with parents, caretakers, and one another in order to ensure that young learners get the most out of their music experiences.

Early childhood music programs that take into account MENC's PreK Standards for Music Education and PreK Opportunity-to-Learn Standards provide a positive and highly beneficial learning environment that will prepare young children for future music learning. These standards can be found in the MENC brochure *Prekindergarten Music Education Standards.*[1] Appropriate methods of assessing preK music learning are addressed in *Performance Standards for Music, Grades PreK–12.*[2]

The articles presented in *Spotlight on Early Childhood Music Education* will support teachers' efforts toward helping their students meet the preK standards. The first section of the book provides an overview of several approaches to early childhood music education. Authors look at the ideas of Gordon, Kodály, Orff, and others who have influenced the field of early childhood music education.

The second section of the book offers various types of musical activities that can be used with young children. The activities expose children to the language of music and inspire creativity and the enjoyment of music.

Spotlight on Early Childhood Music Education ends with two articles about assessment—a topic that is important to the success of any early childhood music program. Authors of both articles stress the value of assessment in the early years and provide suggestions for effective assessment.

It is hoped that this book will serve as a resource for early childhood music educators and that it will inspire further sharing among those in the profession. Our knowledge about children—the way that they learn and the impact that music can have on their young lives—continues to grow. Music educators must continue to carry on a dialog that fuels this progress.

Notes

1. MENC: The National Association for Music Education (Reston, VA: MENC, 1995). Standards for Music Education can also be found in *The School Music Program: A New Vision* (Reston, VA: MENC, 1994) and the Opportunity-to-Learn standards can be found in *Opportunity-to-Learn Standards for Music Instruction, Grades PreK–12* (Reston, VA: MENC, 1994).

2. MENC (Reston, VA: MENC, 1996).

Section 1

 Approaches

Philosophies of early childhood music education abound. Many educators incorporate elements of various methods into their teaching. In this section, authors take a look at several practices that have influenced early childhood music education.

 Section 1

Approaches

Kindermusik
by Kimberly Denney

Kindermusik is an early childhood music and movement program for children ages birth to seven years and their families. Kindermusik is based on the firm belief that every child is musical, the parent is the child's most important teacher, and the home is the most important place for learning to take root and grow. Created by early childhood music educators and informed by the latest research in child development, Kindermusik programs provide early childhood learning opportunities through innovative music and movement curricula and involve families in the joy of their child's development. Kindermusik curricula are designed to be developmentally appropriate—each child is encouraged to learn at his or her own pace. The most current research on child development indicates that a child's fundamental learning takes place between birth and seven years.

Kindermusik offers children a broad array of activities to promote language development, social interaction, cognitive development, coordination, and to awaken a child's imagination.

All Kindermusik curricula include "At Home" materials that are unique to each curriculum. These "At Home" materials extend musical activities from class into the home and encourage parental involvement throughout the week and following years. The core belief of the Kindermusik approach is that musical learning is more than just music alone.

The Kindermusik Foundations of Learning are insights stated throughout the curricula that lead educators and families to understand the many-layered benefits that participation in a Kindermusik class offers. Based on current research, music nurtures a child's cognitive, emotional, social, language and physical development.

Kindermusik Curricula is Developmentally Appropriate

There are four studio curricula in the Kindermusik program:

- Kindermusik Village® for children birth to 18 months;
- Kindermusik Our Time™ for children 18 months to 3 years;
- Growing With Kindermusik® for children 3 to 5 years; and
- Kindermusik for the Young Child® for children 4 to 7 years.

Based on Current Research in Child Development

Kindermusik is eclectic in its incorporation of ideas from the leading approaches and philosophies that influence early childhood music and movement education. The philosophies of Orff, Kodály, Laban, and Dalcroze have helped form the music and movement education foundation upon which the Kindermusik curricula have been built. Kindermusik's strong emphasis on childhood development continues to be shaped by the wisdom of experts like Piaget, Montessori, Greenspan and Brazelton.

Kindermusik also remains current on the ideas promoted by such organizations as Zero to Three, the National Association for the Education of Young Children (NAEYC), MENC: The National Association for Music Education, and the Music Teachers National Association (MTNA). In addition, Kindermusik goes one step further by maintaining an active consultancy on an ongoing basis with experts who inform and endorse the work and research Kindermusik is doing.

That group includes specialists such as Dr. Melissa Johnson, pediatric psychologist; Mr. Arthur Joseph, leading authority on the human voice; Dr. Carla Hannaford, author of *Smart Moves,* Dr. Dan

DeJoy, speech-language pathologist; Claudia Quigg, executive director of BabyTALK; and Anne Green Gilbert, author of *Creative Dance for All Ages,* just to name a few.

A recent research study conducted in 1999 at Sam Houston State University on the benefits of early music education focused on Kindermusik and the results suggest that early music training can improve intelligence but the amount of parental involvement in the music training can greatly affect the amount of improvement. Results of this study appeared in the fall 1999 *Journal of Applied Developmental Psychology* that was published in December 1999.

This study has shown very compelling results that early music education improves children's intelligence, without respect to socio-economic or ethnic status. Equally compelling is the study's conclusion that parent involvement in the child's learning experience was the most significant predictor of the amount of improvement in intelligence scoring—over and above parental education level, income level, single/dual parent household or ethnic/minority status.

Kindermusik University Offers a Self-Paced Learning Environment for Educators

Educators who are interested in becoming trained to teach Kindermusik may enroll in Kindermusik University. Kindermusik University (KU) offers the opportunity for prospective educators to become trained and licensed by taking course work via a series of home-based workbooks and videos with the aid of web-site support and e-mail communication with masterful Kindermusik educators and peers.

In summary, a gentle mixture of music and movement enhances a child's learning. Kindermusik provides a unique experience for families and a fulfilling career for music educators.

Kimberly Denney is a Kindermusik teacher and regional advisor for Kindermusik International in Ohio. This is an excerpt from an article that originally appeared in the September-October 2000 issue of Ohio's Triad. *Reprinted by permission.*

Musikgarten®: A Music and Movement Program for Young Children and Their Families
by Dorothy Simonis Denton

In 1994, Lorna Lutz Heyge and Audrey Sillick founded a revolutionary early childhood music education company, after over 25 years of experience with music and movement in early childhood. Musikgarten® is a realization of a dream and a life's work for these collaborators. Through education, studio support, and quality materials and instruments, their company is designed to enable teachers to understand how children from birth to age seven learn music and give them the tools to help children on every level, physically, socially, cognitively and emotionally.

Anyone who is interested in early childhood music will be familiar with the standard "tools of the trade": scarves, wood sticks, jingles, hoops, drums, resonator bars, etc., that are in the Musikgarten teacher's classroom. To the observer, the baby singing their "first language," the gentle floating of a scarf by a toddler, or the solfège work of a sweet singing six-year-old can seem like magic. The "magic" is simply a well-integrated curriculum, delivered by teachers who are enthusiastic and trained by some of the best in the field. They know that a meaningful experience includes an inviting, non-judgmental environment, well-planned music and movement activities that call for response, and a caring parent.

The emphasis on ongoing teacher training is one of the special features of this methodology/business; it facilitates the goal of quality music experiences to as many children as possible, in a society that has *lots* of recorded music but where children have little opportunity to experience or move to live music.

Training helps the teacher understand how music prepares the child's ear, voice, and body to listen and integrate the experience. Best of all, it encourages the teachers to become observers of children and witnesses to the joy that music can bring into life and family relationships.

Philosophy
At the core of the curriculum is a solid philosophy grounded by the influences of Orff, Dalcroze, Laban, and Gordon. The emphasis is on aural and rhythmic preparation, singing, breathing, active quiet listening, and rhythmic movement. In short,

the making of music prepares children bodily and lays the groundwork for eventual reading, writing, and improvisation.

In great evidence is the influence of the educator, Dr. Maria Montessori, the influence of ear research by Alfred Tomatis and the impact of neuroscience educators such as Dee Coulter. The list could go on and on...poetry by Aileen Fisher, original music by Howard Baer, the rich amount of traditional songs, nature themes...The beauty of the curriculum is in the intertwining of all these threads and the ways we encourage very young children to join in the tapestry making. The Musikgarten curriculum is a work in progress, constantly open to new colors and design, and yet well supported.

The invitation to music work must come from a joyful teacher who understands the way young children learn and can adapt quickly to their needs. Teachers, like most students, need the freedom to be themselves to reach their full potential. Musikgarten provides both the freedom and the guidance necessary through flexible curriculum and wonderful training opportunities. Music teachers often already come to training with a great respect for the children's contributions. The trainers show you how to engage the children in a dynamic learning process and help the children form a basis for a life-long love of music. When this involves the parents, also, the music becomes a binding force.

"Families are searching for ways to interact with their children—frankly, ways to compete with television and the other influences in their young children's lives. This program does just that. It engages parent and child in a musical encounter that is play for children now and learning for the rest of life," explains Lorna Heyge.

The authors feel that their emphasis on ear training, purposeful movement, the singing voice, melodic and rhythm patterning and basic instrument work give the children the holistic experiences they need. These form the warp for a child's knowledge and they are the constants in *all* the classes, whether you are teaching "Family Music for Babies or Toddlers,"® "The Cycles of Seasons"® for 3-4 year olds, the "Music Makers"® class of 4-6 year olds, or "Music Makers at the Keyboard"® for 6–8 year olds. Slowly, as the children develop, the moving, listening, and singing "spiral" challenges them at each step. Each child, though, has the freedom to respond in his/her own way, developing an innate aptitude.

The framework, basic lesson plans, encourages the artistic nature of the child. It has a positive, highly significant impact on children's development, which is measurable. Besides nurturing children's social skills through music (most teachers see improvement in self-confidence), body awareness, social awareness, abstract thinking, and improvisation at many levels are also impacted.

This is greatly supported by family involvement. Music, when it involves the family, allows the music to have a "feeling base" that connects it to an emotional sharing. It's evident that the music experiences shared in class bond families together and enrich whole communities! It's very evident that this involvement solidifies the experiences in the young child's heart, where it is treasured.

In Conclusion

Musikgarten can be applied anywhere there are interested children. Teachers are free to take the program to daycares, church choirs, pre-schools, private schools, studio settings, early intervention programs, etc.

For people who wish to offer something unique for children in a summer program, Musikgarten has several offerings. "Nature's Music"® for 2-3 year olds and "Nature Trail,"® a summer experience for the 4–7 crowd.

In summary, Musikgarten as a curriculum is a bountiful musical garden that will continue to nourish children for as long as there are teachers to cultivate.

Dorothy Simonis Denton directs a Musikgarten-dedicated studio in Mansfield, Ohio. This is an excerpt from an article that originally appeared in the September-October 2000 issue of Ohio's Triad. *Reprinted by permission.*

Music for Babies: A New Twist on an Old Idea
by Jill Hannagan

I recently had lunch with my 80-year-old mother and two of her friends. In an attempt to find something interesting to chat about I told them about a large "gathering drum" I had ordered to use in my "Music for Babies" class. One of the women asked what age children I teach, but before I could answer my mother said, "Babies! She teaches babies! Can you imagine? People actually bring their babies to her for music class! What in the world do you teach babies?!?"

This is an especially interesting question to be coming from my mother since she has spent her entire life teaching music. (In fact, she is a member of the DMEA Hall of Fame!) Even at age 80, she directs a gospel choir at her local senior center! But it is a perfectly reasonable question, and one that deserves some discussion. This is a very exciting time to be involved in music education. Recent research has revealed so much about how we learn in general, and more specifically, how we learn music. We no longer proceed on the premise that a few chosen people are talented and the rest of us would be better off to confine our singing to the shower. We now know that all of us are born with an aptitude for music, and that music aptitude, like intelligence, is normally distributed. We also know that music aptitude diminishes if it is not nurtured by early and repeated appropriate experiences. This means that a person's ability to fulfill his music potential is determined by both his innate music aptitude and the quality of his early music experiences.

We also know that we learn music the same way we learn language. Therefore, if we examine the way a child learns the language of his culture, we will have a guide as to what is an appropriate early-childhood music experience.

Using fiber optic cameras, Dr. Alfred Tomatis discovered that a five-month old fetus is capable of hearing and responding to the sounds of language. This means that babies are absorbing the sounds and rhythms of their native language from as early as five months in utero. Since most children do not begin to speak until sometime near the end of their first year, it is safe to say that they were bathed in the sounds and rhythms of their language for well over a year before actually being expected to speak.

They will then spend many months experimenting with isolated words, eventually combining them to make phrases. With the passage of even more time, they will be able to speak in complete sentences. All the while, we continue to bathe them in language, never considering the idea of "holding out on them" until they are ready to answer us in complete sentences. It is the very fact that we continue to talk to them, regardless of their ability to respond, that allows children to become fluent in language. In this sense, children are not taught language; they acquire language when:

a. they have a strong aural foundation made up of their sensory experiences while in utero and during the first few years of life
b. they are given ample time to organize and assimilate those experiences
c. the sensory experiences have an emotional component

In a 1997 special edition of *Newsweek* devoted to brain development, Janellen Hullocher of the University of Chicago suggests that "Information embedded in an emotional context seems to stimulate neural circuitry more powerfully than information alone." This idea is substantiated by neuropsychologist and educator, Carla Hannaford, Ph.D., who states in her book, *Smart Moves: Why Learning is Not All in Your Head,* "In order to learn something, there must be sensory input, a personal emotional connection, and movement...Emotions interpret each experience and help us to organize it in terms of our view of the world."

From this information we can conclude that live music-making provides the child with a much richer sensory and emotional experience than recorded music could ever hope to. In fact, it's hard to imagine a more sensorially and emotionally charged experience than that of a mother singing to and dancing with her child. The baby is not only hearing her voice, he is feeling the vibration of her voice as his head rests on her chest, he smells the familiar scent of her body, while all the while his vestibular system is being stimulated by the rocking, bouncing, and spinning of their dance. This is a far cry from a baby lying in his crib listening to a cassette.

So in answer to my mother's question, "What in the world do you teach babies?" I would have to say: The goal of all parent/child music classes should not be to teach anything! Rather, it should be to guide parents and children as they engage in musical activities that will help the child fulfill his music potential; to bathe them in the sounds and rhythms of the music of our culture; to provide an environment which encourages musical interaction between parents and children, and gives parents the chance to get ideas from other parents as they make music with their children; to guide parents as to what movements are most beneficial for development; to pass on the songs and rhymes that are part of our cultural heritage; and to add to the collection of emotional, sensory experiences that will make up the aural foundation on which all future music learning will be based.

Having said all that, my primary goal for both the parents and children in my classes is that they experience the joy of making music with others.

The feeling created by engaging in active music-making with other people is quite special and becomes even more special when experienced by parents and children together. Who knows…perhaps I can talk my mother into joining our class this year!

Jill Hannagan teaches newborns through nine-year-olds at the Hockessin Music School in Hockessin, Delaware. This article originally appeared in the December 1998 issue of Delaware's The DMEA Notes. *Reprinted by permission.*

A Kodály Approach
by Jo Kirk

As early as the 1940's Zoltán Kodály (1882–1967), the Hungarian composer and music educator, had identified the importance of early childhood music education. When asked when early music education should begin he answered "nine months before the birth of the mother." At that time he stated:

> Recent psychology has set forth convincingly that the years between birth and seven are educationally much more important than the later ones. What is spoiled or omitted at this age cannot be put right later on. In these years man's future is decided practically for his whole lifetime.[1]

Current research in early brain development and music learning theory strongly support Kodály's convictions.

Philosophy
Singing is the child's main mode of musical participation and provides the basis for musical development. Katalin Forrai, a leading Hungarian early childhood music specialist states,

> The elements of music should be distilled from live music and singing; the children should themselves recognize basic musical concepts through…experiencing the games and singing the songs.

As the child sings the voice is explored and comfort in singing is gained. In an environment rich with singing the child develops a musical ear, begins to match pitch, and sings in tune.

The song repertoire is built on the traditional children's folk song, nursery rhyme, and singing game. Kodály defined the folk song as the best music to use in early childhood because it encompasses the criteria for the selection of quality children's music literature. Rhythmically and melodically the folk song closely correlates to the natural rhythms and contours of the spoken language.

Dr. John Feierabend, director of the Music Education Division at The Hartt School of the University of Hartford and director of the National Center for Music and Movement in the Early Years, states, "The marriage of words and the melody in a children's song should embody all the subtleties of natural spoken inflection."[3] The folk song text speaks of the child's world of wonder and make believe and reflects the child's interests and concerns. Folk song literature has stood the test of time and continues to bring long-lasting joy to the adult and child alike, even after numerous repetitions.

Singing does not stand alone. Kodály points out, "Singing is the instinctive language of the child, and the younger he is the more he requires movement to go with it."[4]

Movement is the child's most favorite response to music. Music and movement are inseparable in early childhood. Grasping this concept, Kodály was greatly influenced by the work of Dalcroze. Through movement the child experiences and gains a better understanding of beat, rhythm, melodic contour, tempo, and form which in turn can stimulate the child's musical sensitivity and creativity.

Goals

1. *To awaken the child's desire for music and foster the joys it brings.*

Childhood is life's first gift and we should encourage the child to play it for all it's worth. Kodály pointed out, "The longer the childhood is, the more harmonious and happier the adult life will be."[5]

The child explores a variety of musical concepts in a joyful, playful atmosphere. Informal, playful instruction brings skill development and joy to the learning experience. Forrai affirms the importance of joy. "More important even than musical consideration are the joys of singing, the pleasure of the game, and the group experience. This true spirit of play will eventually have a positive influence on the achievement of musical goals."[6]

2. *To nurture the child's innate musical intelligence, therefore laying a firm foundation for later musical studies and participation.*

Musical skills are developed in a stimulating environment of singing, moving, playing simple instruments, chanting, creating, and exploring musical concepts. Unconsciously, melodic and rhythmic concepts are understood and the child begins to use them in his music making.

3. *To foster parent-child interaction, parent-child education.*

The parent is the child's first teacher and the home is the first school. The research of Jenkins (1976) and Kirkpatrick (1962) confirmed the importance of the home environment and parent model in the development of the child's musical behavior.[7] The enthusiasm and participation of the parent is paramount.

Children are aware of the adults' interests, moods, and behaviors. As the parent engages in musical activities with the child, the child begins to model musical interest and demonstrate their love for music. Edwin Gordon emphasizes the importance of a home environment rich in music. "The effect of a rich home environment on a child's music aptitude decreases at an increasing rate as the child grows older. The importance of an early and rich music environment cannot be over estimated."[8]

4. *To enhance and refine non-music skills essential to the child's healthy development.*

The element of play is found in music activities. It acts as a positive motivator toward the development of vital nonmusic skills. Musical play provides quality repetition instead of drill; therefore, the child develops motor, social, language, cognitive, listening, and creative skills in a joyful, playful atmosphere where he thinks he is playing but we know he is learning.

Curriculum Development

The basic curriculum is designed around the passive and active learning stages as defined by John Feierabend.[9] During the passive stage, birth to approximately eighteen months, the parent needs to do things to, for, and with the child to bring him/her to the musical stimulation and experience. The song material falls into the categories, labeled by Feierabend, of bounces, wiggles, tickles, taps, claps, movement to recording, easy-to-sing songs, lullabies, and songs for listening.[10]

The child takes on a more active role in the music class at approximately nineteen months through five years of age. The categories for the song material used during the active learning stage are finger plays, action songs, pitch exploration, easy-to-sing songs, creating, movement exploration, independent singing, moving to classical recordings, and songs for listening.[11]

The Teacher

"A child will learn anything if there is somebody who knows how to teach him."[12] It is essential that the teacher demonstrate artful teaching skills and excellent personal musicianship.

In Conclusion

Language skills are developed as the child is immersed in an environment rich in speech, reading, and conversation, in the same way musical skills are developed when the child is surrounded by quality musical experiences during the early years. The foundation of this experience is experience in singing. Its expressive powers and joyful nature bring the child to musical understanding and lays the foundation for musical literacy. Something special happens between those who share music together. As we sing together, these words take on a deeper meaning, "The more we get together, the happier we'll be."

Notes

1. Zoltán Kodály, *The Selected Writings of Zoltán Kodály* (London: Boosey and Hawkes, 1974), 129.

2. Katalin Forrai, Music in Preschool (Budapest: Corvina Press, 1988), 33.

3. John Feierabend, "Music and Movement for Infants and Toddlers: Naturally Wonder-Full," *Early Childhood Connections* 2, no. 4 (1996): 21.

4. Zoltán Kodály, *Singing Games* in *The Selected Writings of Zoltán Kodály* (London: Boosey and Hawkes, 1974).

5. Zoltán Kodály, *Viszatekintes* (Memories), (Budapest: Corvina Press), 62f.

6. Katalin Forrai, *Music in Preschool* (Budapest: Corvina Press, 1988), 27.

7. J. Jenkins, "The relationship between maternal parents' musical experience and the musical development of two- and three-year-old girls" (Ann Arbor, MI: University Microfilms, 1976) and W. Kirkpatrick, "Relationships between the singing ability of pre-kindergarten children and their home musical environment" (Ann Arbor, MI: University Microfilms, 1962), cited in Donna B. Fox, "MusicTIME and Music Times Two: The Eastman Infant-Toddler Music Program," in *Promising Practices: Prekindergarten Music Education* (Reston: Music Educators National Conference, 1989), 13.

8. Edwin Gordon, *A Music Learning Theory for Newborn and Young Children* (Chicago: G.I.A. Press, 1990), 10.

9. John Feierabend, "Music and Movement for Infants and Toddlers: Naturally Wonder-Full," *Early Childhood Connections* 2, no. 4 (1996): 23.

10. John Feierabend, *Music for Very Little People, 50 Playful Activities for Infants and Toddlers* (London: Boosey and Hawkes, 1986).

11. John Feierabend, *Music for Little People, 50 Playful Activities for Preschool and Early Elementary School Children* (London: Boosey and Hawkes, 1989).

12. Zoltán Kodály, *The Selected Writings of Zoltán Kodály* (London: Boosey and Hawkes, 1974), 149.

Jo Kirk is a Kodály training teacher and founder and director of WeJoySing—an early childhood music and movement program based in Ohio. This article originally appeared in the April 2000 issue of Ohio's Triad. *Reprinted by permission.*

The Importance of Child Development in Music Education
by Lili M. Levinowitz and Ann Adalist-Estrin

The notion of a collaboration with early childhood experts is not a new one. Music activities with preschool children have been promoted for centuries. At the Music in Early Childhood Conference (Provo, Utah, 1984), music educators and early childhood educators worked together to explore the place of music in early child development. One of the tenets that emerged from that conference was that children are biologically "wired" to respond most to those with whom they have a bond of attachment (Katz & Hoffman, 1985). There is also an explosion of data related to early brain growth and developmental implications of this growth to a wide variety of disciplines.

As we move into the 21st century then, it is of utmost importance to recognize the role of the parent-child relationships and the overall developmental context of the child's first years. Creating a philosophy and pedagogy from the existing sources in both music and child development will help educators to design new models for the inclusion of music in the very early years.

This is not always an easy task. These are confusing times in which to nourish the hearts, minds, and talents of young children. Much information is available to us, but gone are the days of right answers, leading experts, and linear causal patterns. True, competing philosophies have always jockeyed for a place as the favored theory. Some of those theories provided answers for a period of time until another theory, with its answers, replaced it. Not so long ago for example, it was a generally accepted notion that children didn't really learn until they went to school (music in particular) and that babies could neither see nor hear at birth (much less sing). It was a time when Spock ruled if you had a question about child development. That is, there was really only one source to head for and the correct answer would await you.

Today, the adults who are responsible for making decisions for their young children are faced with an onslaught of information on child rearing. Just browse your local bookstore to find experts expounding on every topic from toilet training to beginning music lessons. Look more closely, and you'll find that these experts often represent divergent opinions. This opinion cornucopia is creating a shift for parents and teachers from depending on right answers from the leaders in the field to crafting a perspective of their own by combining ideas from existing information.

While parents and teachers struggle with the absence of a single answer to bridge music and child development, there are emerging principles that can guide us. It is important to look with some detail to the aspects of growth and development that are considered most significant: Endowment/maturation (musical and non-musical); Developmental process (language, cognition, motor, psycho-social, musical); Temperament relationships/attachments.

Maturation and Development

At birth, a child's biological endowment, both musical and non-musical, is the result of the combination of genetics and interuterine/birth experience influences. This gives the child not only his/her limbs for creative movement, a larynx for singing, and sensory systems for assimilating his/her surroundings, but also the capacity for organizing experiences and interacting with the environment (Fenichel, Pawl and Williamson, 1996). The development process unfolds these inherent capacities into skills that are observable at an expected rate and sequence. It is this developmental timetable that signals a child to walk, move to a beat, sing in tune, and share toys or read. It is environmental factors that support or delay the development of these skills once they have begun. The importance of environmental factors in music development is supported by the case study undertaken by Kelley and Sutton-Smith (1987). They studied three first-born females from birth to two years of age who were reared in families with three contrasting musical backgrounds. One set of parents were professional musicians, another set were musically oriented but not practicing professional musicians, and the final set were not musically oriented and hence made fewer musical choices in their child rearing practices. The differences between family number three, who was not musically oriented and the other two families were startling in that the two children who had a sufficiency in their musical environment were considerably more developed in their music behaviors.

Outside of music, the way children have been viewed, understood and evaluated in the early years has been primarily focused on the maturational and developmental factors. Psychologists and pediatricians often use a specific aspect of development as a lens for viewing the child's overall functioning. In infancy, motor skills are most often the gauge; dur-

ing the toddler years, language is the window into a child's growth. This leads to a focus on cognitive ability in the preschool years and finally, psychosocial behaviors in school-age children.

Much of what these researchers and clinicians have looked at and for in all of these categories has been based on the work of Jean Piaget making it clear that some old answers have endured (Piaget, 1966). The following explanation can begin to build the bridge between music and child development.

Piaget's theory suggests that children develop their ability to learn, think and reason both musically and non-musically as they progress through a series of developmental stages each marked by an increased ability to be logical and comprehend the abstract. He identified practice and imitation as the primary tools for learning at each stage of this process (Greenspan, 1979).

The infants take the information through all five senses while learning to regulate their bodies and emotional reactions to sensory and environmental input. Babies in the first year prefer to practice and imitate in surroundings that are new and interesting. They thrive on the invitation to explore that which new sights and sounds bring. Their ability to enjoy novelty and successfully explore new surroundings is dependent, however, on the security that comes from significant others; mom, dad or caregiver act as a base from which baby can try out new experiences. Attachment disruptions in the primary relationships can occur for many reasons and create obstacles to the infant's drive to explore and subsequently learn. Involving parents and caregivers in the infant's learning environments and understanding the dynamics of these relationships is essential for providing the basis of support for infant exploration.

Toddlers in contrast, are frightened by change. They crave repetition and ritual. They enjoy singing the same songs over and over, or hearing the same book read many times. Lullabies at bedtime are easily incorporated into their nightly routine. Now children's practice is focused on physical, emotional and intellectual independence from parents and teachers/caregivers; the repetition gives them a safe structure on which to learn to be autonomous. Also, at this time their motor skills refine and combine with language ability and they develop skills in holding images mentally or remembering in pictures, so this is a time when "out of sight" is definitely not "out of mind."

While preschoolers continue to refine sensory motor skills, they now begin to incorporate mental symbols in their language and in their play. Thinking and reasoning moves into the realm of representation and includes much fantasy. The line between fantasy and reality, however, is often blurred. Three-, four- and five-year-olds can now imitate things that are no longer visible and can use objects in creative and symbolic ways. They can imagine a scarf as a branch or a goodbye song as a bon voyage gift. Adults must be cautioned here because preschool children still possess limited understanding of time, space and causality. They can link events that are unrelated and make inferences and draw conclusions that are inaccurate but often sound clear and convincing. If a child has a conflict with another child over a toy or prop during a specific song, he/she may avoid or refuse that song in the future—illogically linking the song with the event.

Clearly the aforementioned biological and maturational abilities converge with these developmental and cognitive processes to form a basic outline for the child's self. Temperament, or a blend of specific behavioral qualities color in that outline and further define a child's learning style.

Temperament

Chess and Thomas (1984) identified nine temperament characteristics that were not clearly linked to child maturation and development in an attempt to offer insight into the variation in child behavior. These qualities affect not only children's behavior but the responses of the adults around them and also the child's internal reaction to his or her body and the environment.

Temperament Characteristics

Rhythmicity is the degree of predictability and rhythm in the timing of biological functions.

Activity Level refers to the motor component of the child's functioning.

Approach/Withdrawl refers to the nature of the child's response to situations which can be modified.

Adaptability is the ease with which a child's response to situations can be modified.

Threshold of Responsiveness refers to the intensity of stimulation that is necessary to evoke a discernable response from the child.

Intensity of Reaction is the energy level of the child's response to stimuli.

Quality of Mood is a term for the overall positive or negative tone of the child's behavior.

Distractibility is the ease with which a child can be diverted from ongoing activity by extraneous peripheral stimuli.

Attention Span and Persistence refer to both the length of time a child will pursue a particular activity and the continued interest in that activity in the face of obstacles.

While the temperament characteristics themselves are not necessarily fixed, they do present behaviors that are likely to persist over time based on the fit between the child and parents/caregivers (Carey and McDevitt, 1997; Greenspan, 1995). Derived from a variety of constitutional and environmental factors, temperament might be described as the "how" of development, maturation as the "what," and relationships as the "why."

Relationships/Attachments

Several decades ago, British pediatrician and psychiatrist, Donald Winnicot, shocked his colleagues, by suggesting that there was no such a thing as a baby —only a baby and a caregiver together (Winnicot, 1986). This comment heralded the beginning of a reframing of child development observations from "child focused" to a model that viewed children's progress in the context of their social relationships. This recognizes the fundamental power of significant relationships as the fuel for growth or the "why" of behavior (Adalist-Estrin, 1996).

Connections between maturation, development and relationships occur throughout childhood. Newest data on brain development indicates that parents' responses to child behavior as well as the overall quality of the parent-child relationship affects not only attachment and emotional development (Mahler, 1975; Brazelton and Cramer, 1990) but also the child's central nervous system and self-regulatory abilities (Haffer, 1996). When parents are chronically unable to read their children's signals or respond to them with understanding, awareness and sensitivity, the damage to brain development may be difficult to repair in later life. Studies on a wide range of children who have suffered trauma or loss confirm these findings (Doolittle, 1995; Osborne, 1995; Terr, 1990). It is clear that children are motivated by their relationships to parents or significant teachers/caregivers. Moreover, parents' participation in their child's learning process is positively correlated with achievement.

Parents do bring a host of feelings and needs, though, that may interfere with their ability to interact with their children and support their learning. Temperament and style differences as well as performance expectations can affect the parents' responses to an individual child or a particular developmental task. In short, parents may sometimes have difficulty accepting their child's abilities, limitations and needs. What usually interferes, however, is their desire to raise competent children and to get feedback from those around them about their parenting!

Fortunately, many of the models for preschool music experiences include the parent. As these models evolve they should create a new arena of learning for music teachers. That is, music educators must begin to understand the impact that parents have on their child's music learning and the effect the child's behavior has on the parents' feelings. This is a new role for music teachers in early childhood to serve as an objective facilitator when normal parent/child conflicts present themselves, to respond to emotions of parents, and to act as a buffer when parent/child relationship conflicts interfere in music learning activities. When, however, teachers acknowledge the parents' fears and needs in addition to communicating developmentally appropriate expectations, parents feel understood and can more easily accept their child's skills.

We now know that young children are indeed competent learners, coming to the world with dramatically developed skills. Brain scan research confirms that young children's brains are twice as active than those of adults (Chugani, 1996). This supports the notion that early stimulation is essential for not only affecting mood, but also to affect how the brain is wired. In addition, we are learning that the quality of the parent/child relationship is related to optimal brain development (Carnegie, 1994). Music and its nearly universal appeal to parents and children alike create an atmosphere and a context for the development of attachment.

Whenever a mother sings a lullaby to her child, or a dad pats to the beat of a chant while changing a baby's diaper or caregivers use musical tones to babble call and response games, they are providing…

- Sensory stimulation in the context of a loving environment.
- Rich and valuable language and musical experiences.
- An opportunity to learn about this child's temperament and skills.
- Practice for their child's use of imitation and the mastery of skills.
- Memories of music as a positive source of nurturance.

Parents most often need only to know that they are competent at providing these experiences. The role of the music educators in supporting and fostering this competence by involving parents, teaches them about their children while acknowledging their fears and concerns. This not only fosters musical abilities but also contributes significantly to the overall growth and development of the child.

References

Adalist-Estrin, A. (1996). Relationships are the key to development." In *Putting healthy steps into practice: Healthy steps training manual.* Boston: Boston University School of Medicine.

Brazelton, T. B. & Cramer, B. G. (1990). *The earliest relationship: Parents, infants and the drama of early attachment.* Reading, MA: Addison-Wesley.

Carey, W. B. & McDevitt, S. C. (1995). *Coping with children's temperament: Guide for professionals.* New York: Basic Books.

Carnegie Task Force on Meeting the Needs of our Youngest Children. (1994). *Starting points: Meeting the needs of our youngest children.* New York: Carnegie Corporation of New York.

Chess, S. & Thomas, A. (1984). *Origins and evaluation of behavior disorders: From infancy to adult life.* New York: Bruner-Mazel.

Chugani, H. T. (In Press). Neuroimaging of developmental and non-linear and developmental pathologic. In R. W. Thatcher, G. R. Lyon, J. Rumsey & N. Krosnegor (Eds.), *Developmental neuroimaging: Mapping the development of brain and behavior.*

Doolittle, T. (1995). *The long term effects of institutionalization on the behavior of children from Eastern Europe and the Former Soviet Union.* Meadowlands, PA: Parent Network for Post-Institutionalized Children.

Fenichel, E., Pawl, J., & Williamson, G. (1996). "The first three years: Overview of the developing child." In *Putting healthy steps into practice: Healthy steps training manual.* Boston: University School of Medicine.

Greenspan, S. I. (1995). *The challenging child.* Reading, MA: Wesley-Addison.

Greenspan, S. I. (1979). *Intelligence and adaption.* New York: International Universities Press.

Haffer, M. A. (1996). "Hidden regulators: Implications for a new understanding of attachment, separation and loss." In S. Goldberg, R. Meur and J. Kerr (Eds.), *Attachment theory: Social development and clinical perspectives.* Hillside, New Jersey: The Analytic Press.

Katz, L. & M. E. Hoffman (1985). "Recent research on young children: Implications for teaching and development implications for music education." In J. Boswell (Ed.), *The young child and music: Contemporary principles in child development and music education* (pp. 83–90). Reston, VA: MENC.

Kelley & Sutton-Smith (1987) in *Music and child development.* New York: Springer- Verlag.

Mahler, M., Pine, F., & Bergman, A. (1975). *Psychological birth of the human infant: Symbiosis and individuation.* New York: Basic Books.

Osborne, L. (1995). Parental depression. In B. Zuckerman, & S. Parker (Eds.), *Developmental and behavioral pediatrics.* Boston: Little Brown.

Piaget, J. (1966). *The psychology of the child.* New York: Little Brown.

Terr, L.T. (1990). *Too scared to cry: Psychic trauma in childhood.* New York: Harper and Row.

Winnicot, D. (1986). The Newborn and His Mother. In C. Winnicot, et. al. (Eds.), *Babies and their mothers.* Reading, MA: Addison-Wesley.

Lili M. Levinowitz is professor of music education at Rowan University in New Jersey, and Ann Adalist-Estrin is a child and family therapist consultant and trainer in Philadelphia, Pennsylvania. This article originally appeared in the October 1999 issue of New Jersey's Tempo. *Reprinted by permission.*

Music Together
by Lili M. Levinowitz and Kenneth K. Guilmartin

Music Together is a music and movement approach to early childhood music development for infant, toddler, preschool, and kindergarten children and their parents, teachers, and other primary caregivers. Originally offered to the public in 1987 it pioneered the concept of a research-based, developmentally appropriate early childhood music curriculum that strongly emphasizes and facilitates adult involvement.

The *Music Together* approach develops every child's birthright of basic music competence by encouraging the actual experiencing of music rather than the learning of concepts or information about music. It began as an educational project of the Center for Music and Young Children and is now being taught nationwide. *Music Together* tapes, song books, and classroom techniques enjoy widespread use by teachers and families both directly and indirectly involved in *Music Together.*

The Center for Music and Young Children (CMYC), developer of *Music Together*, was founded in 1985. CMYC is committed to helping families, caregivers, and early childhood professionals rediscover the pleasure and educational value of informal musical experiences. Rather than emphasizing traditional music performances, CMYC encourages family participation in spontaneous musical activity occurring within the context of daily life. CMYC recognizes that all children are musical and that every child needs a stimulating, supportive music environment to achieve basic competence in the wonderful human capacity for music-making.

Music Together is:

Music and movement for families:
- Infants/Toddlers/Preschoolers
- parent/child classes with parent education
- music learned through playful activities in mixed-age classes
- developmentally appropriate and research-based

Music for preschools and daycare centers:
- staff involvement, regardless of musical ability
- parent involvement

Family and classroom-tested materials:
- tapes, CDs, song books, and instrument-play materials
- parent/caregiver education

Teacher Training and Support
- Music Educators/Preschool Teachers/Daycare Providers/Parents

Song Collections
CMYC has developed many song collections containing fun, simple, musically interesting songs,

both traditional and original, that will appeal to the whole family. The music is pitched in just the right range for children's voices and includes songs (with and without words), rhythmic chants, tonal and rhythm patterns, and instrumental "play-alongs," all in a rich variety of tonalities and meters. Outstanding instrumentalists are recorded playing a variety of instruments.

The song collections, including song books, CDs, and tapes, are designed to be used consecutively, one each semester. The collections are suitable for mixed-age groups, so that daycare centers and families with children of different ages can enjoy the same music.

The song collections are research-based, artistically conceived and produced, and are classroom- and family-tested. The feedback of hundreds of teachers and thousands of families over more than ten years has been incorporated in these constantly evolving materials.

Music Together® Materials and Rhythm Instruments:

Besides the Song Collection CDs, support materials and rhythm instruments are also made available to the parents in the *Music Together* program. For each CD there is a suggested list of materials that may be purchased to use with the CD. For example, the materials suggested for the "Sticks" Song Collection are: rainbow scarf, whale castanets, tymptone drum, egg shakers, rhythm sticks, tambourine, tone block, and jingle taps. Other CD titles in the Song Collection are the "Tambourine" Song Collection and the "Drum" Song Collection.

Regular newsletters keep *Music Together* families on the cutting edge providing news and information for parents and teachers as well as suggested resources and ideas for at-home activities. The newsletters are published at least twice a year.

Music Together is an approach to early childhood music that began as an educational project and has developed into a nationally known organization that brings the whole family together.

Lili M. Levinowitz is professor of music education at Rowan University in New Jersey. Kenneth K. Guilmartin conceived of and developed the Music Together *program for the Center for Music and Young Children which he founded in Princeton, New Jersey, in 1985. This is an excerpt from an article that originally appeared in the September-October 2000 issue of Ohio's* Triad. *Reprinted by permission.*

A Dalcroze Approach
by Nancy E. Lineburgh

You've entered a large room, empty, except for a piano, a teacher, and a small group of preschool children. The children are dressed in leotards or shorts and t-shirts, and are barefoot. As the class begins, the teacher plays enchanting music on the piano and the children run to the music. When the music stops, the children stop; when the teacher plays a graceful turn, the children do a little twirl, then go on. Today the children are leaves in the wind; the wind blows, the children move; they twirl in the wind.

You have entered an enchanting world of music; a world of playfulness and imagination; a world where music and movement mesh to become a means of musical expression for all who participate. This is what people call "Dalcroze."

When people say "Dalcroze" they are referring to a way of teaching music devised by Emile Jaques-Dalcroze (1865–1950), a Swiss musician and teacher who revolutionized music education by introducing the idea that musical concepts could be taught and truly owned through movement activities. Students in Dalcroze classes respond to music through their own natural movements (i.e., walking, running, skipping, stretching, bending, swaying, etc.). The object of this way of teaching is to develop in the student a natural rhythmic sense, musicality, and concentration through movement to music.

The Dalcroze Work
The work of Dalcroze is broken up into three areas: eurhythmics (rhythmic movement), solfège (singing using do, re, mi, fa, so, la, ti, do), and improvisation (music that is created spontaneously without any musical notation). The word "eurhythmics" comes from Greek with the "eu" meaning "good," and the "rhythmics" meaning "rhythm," thus meaning "good rhythm."

While training programs for adults often segregate the three areas of study (eurhythmics, solfège, and improvisation), classes for children generally weave these areas together into one class.

The most common age for starting a child in traditional Dalcroze classes is age 3 or 4. The child needs to be willing to generally follow directions, since the classes are teacher directed, although student input is always welcomed and used. The lessons are playful and fun.

At the core of the work are basic rhythmic movements: walk, run, stretch, skip, gallop, and sway. These movements are sometimes put together to create rhythm patterns. Other concepts taught include: tempo, rhythm patterns, meter, phrase and form, pitch and melody, staccato and legato, major and minor, sound and silence, pitch memory, high and low, up and down, accent, mood, and texture. Another aspect of the Dalcroze work, called "plastique," involves simply moving expressively to music.

By experiencing many aspects of music in movement, the child develops a kinesthetic memory for the experience. The memory of the movement and, hopefully, the expressiveness of the movement, can later be called upon when performing music.

Class material is generally created by the teacher and supported with improvised and recorded music. Books listed in this article provide examples of Dalcroze activities especially designed for young children.

Historic Background

Even though the idea of using movement to teach rhythm and musicality came about as an outgrowth of work with college-age students, Dalcroze saw the application of his ideas to young children early on in his career.

> The important thing, as one cannot repeat too often, is that the child should learn to feel music, to absorb it not merely with his ear, but with his whole being. (Jaques-Dalcroze, p. 49)

He also believed that musicality could be taught if the proper methods were used.

> We cannot repeat too often that musical instinct does not always emerge of itself, but requires to be brought out by a training in association of ideas. Twenty years ago I wrote some little songs, and set children to punctuate them with bodily movements. I frequently noticed that children who did not care for music, and detested singing, came to love the songs, through love of the movements. The two essential elements in music are rhythm and sound. Often a taste for rhythmic movement will lead a child, possessing only slight auditive faculties, to appreciate music. (Jaques-Dalcroze, p. 51)

He also understood the importance of exposing the young child to only the best music. "One cannot be too careful in seeing that, from the tenderest age, the child hears only good music." This idea was supported by the philosophy of Rousseau who said, "A man's education commences at his birth." (Jaques-Dalcroze, p. 50)

Regarding the importance of beginning music training at a young age, Dalcroze said,

> I therefore set about training the ears of my pupils as early as possible, and discovered thereby not only that the hearing faculties develop with remarkable ease at a stage when every new sensation delights the child, and stimulates in him a joyful curiosity, but, in addition that once the ear is trained to the natural sequences of sounds and chords, the mind no longer experiences the slightest difficulty in accustoming itself to the various processes of reading and writing. (Jaques-Dalcroze, p. vii)

Arthur Becknell's dissertation entitled *A History of the Development of Dalcroze Eurhythmics in the United States and its Influence on the Public School Music Program* gives some evidence for the existence of children's classes as early as 1906 in Geneva. In the United States, the first children's classes were held during the 1920-1921 school year at The Dalcroze School of Music in New York City.

In Ohio, the most prominent institution supporting the Dalcroze work has been the Cleveland Institute of Music, founded in 1920 by Ernest Bloch. Children's classes started in the 1926–1927 school year. Work with very young children began when Elsa Findlay joined the faculty in 1956. The description of her children's class in the 1957–1958 catalog read:

> A strong foundation in musical rhythm and bodily coordination is imperative for future musical instrumental experiences. Exercises especially designed to meet these objectives are a part of each Eurhythmics lesson. The child becomes sensitive to and aware of variations in tempo, dynamics, and other elements of musical rhythm. Since learning develops best in an atmosphere of freedom rather than of restraint, each lesson becomes a joyous individual experience where the child contributes and shares with the instructor and the group. Children may begin these classes as early as the age of four, and may continue more advanced work each year." (Becknell, p. 58–59)

Books Based on Dalcroze Methodology

Elsa Findlay wrote a wonderful book that provides many excellent and inspired examples of the Dalcroze work as it is applied to young children. Her book is entitled, *Rhythm and Movement: Applications of Dalcroze Eurhythmics* (1971) and has many wonderful photographs of children in action.

Virginia Mead is another prominent Ohioan who has taught young children using the Dalcroze philosophy. Her book is entitled, *Dalcroze Eurhythmics in Today's Music Classroom* (1994). Many of the ideas in this book can be applied to early childhood Dalcroze classes.

The most well-known historic book based on methodology for young children is Heather Gell's *Music, Movement and the Young Child* (first printed in 1949). Ms. Gell is an Australian early childhood educator who became enthralled with the Dalcroze work, studied extensively in London, and then brought what she had learned back to Australia. Her book is full of many wonderful ideas showing ways to work with children in a Dalcroze way.

Conclusion

Even though the Dalcroze work does not usually begin until the age of 3 or 4, experiences with expressive movement can begin in the womb as the mother moves and feels the flow of music. Once the baby is born, the way a parent rocks the baby to sleep can become a musical experience for the child.

Dalcroze said, "What makes music expressive? What gives life to successions of musical sounds? Movement, rhythm. The nuances of rhythm are perceptible simultaneously by the aural and muscular senses." (Jaques-Dalcroze, p. 51)

References

Becknell, Arthur. (1970). *A History of the Development of Dalcroze Eurhythmics in the United States and its Influence on The Public School Music Program.* (Self-published dissertation.)

Gell, Heather. (1949). *Music, Movement and the Young Child.* Sydney: The Australian Publishing Co.

Findlay, Elsa. (1971). *Rhythm and Movement: Applications of Dalcroze Eurhythmics.* Evanston: Summy-Birchard Company.

Jaques-Dalcroze, Emile. (1921/1967). *Rhythm Music and Education.* London: Riverside Press.

Mead, Virginia. (1994). *Dalcroze Eurhythmics in Today's Music Classroom.* New York: Schott.

Nancy Lineburgh teaches grades K–4 in the Nordonia Hills City School District in Ohio and co-directs an early childhood music program for children from birth to age seven. This article originally appeared in the April 2000 issue of Ohio's Triad. *Reprinted by permission.*

An Orff Approach
by Chet-Yeng Loong

Carl Orff (1895–1982) strongly believed that music is for children of all ages and abilities. The greatest gift of the Orff-Schulwerk (Orff work) is the awakening of children's senses and engagement in a total awareness of music. Orff believed that musical experiences must begin early, during the first years of life. He also believed that every child is educable and that unmusical children are very rare.

Historic Background

The origins of the Orff-Schulwerk can be traced back to the 1920's. Orff was inspired by the "New Dance Wave" and by the eurhythmics of Emile Jaques-Dalcroze. Thus, in 1924, he founded the Guenther Schule (a German School) with his colleague, Dorothee Guenther. Here his lifelong interest in children's music education began.

The school provided a setting for musicians and dancers to integrate their arts. They learned to dance, sing, and play musical instruments in order to understand all facets of music. Orff composed music for the Guenther school and designed special instruments which would imitate what he termed the "elemental style," "a music which is not abstract, but which integrates the elements of speech, movement, and dance" (Warner, p. 3). ("Elemental" is a word Orff used to refer to music that is natural to early man and the music of young children.)

Orff was fascinated by the exotic Balinese gamelan and African percussion ensembles. Around 1926 he received a gift of an African xylophone. At the same time, he realized that he needed a tonal, fundamental, primitive instrument for his dancers' orchestra at the Guenther Schule.

The unique instruments Orff designed were barred percussion modeled after Balinese and African xylophones and built to Orff's specification. They included barred instruments xylophones, with wooden timbre; metallophones, with a metal timbre; and glockenspiels, with a bell-like timbre) as well as recorders, small percussion instruments, and drums.

After 1948, Orff was assisted by his former student, Gunild Keetman. They developed and refined the Orff-Schulwerk program and involved children in making and experiencing music. In addition, singing became a more important component in the program. Later, five volumes of *Music for Children* were published. Keetman wrote,

> When 'Music for Children' was first formulated about twenty years ago the work started with children of about seven years old. Now, in line with the most recent knowledge about early education, it often begins in nursery or infant school. (Keetman, 1970).

When the Orff Institute was opened in Salzburg, Austria, in 1963, the intent was to provide training for teachers from preschool through adults. Carl Orff wrote:

> The training in the seminar should enable the student to use the means and method of Elemental Music and Movement Training according to Orff-Schulwerk principles in nursery school (preschool), in general and further education institutions, in professional music and movement studies and also in social and medical training. The institute's children's classes are available to students for teaching practice. (Orff, 1976)

Orff-Schulwerk Philosophy

Orff strongly believed that music is for children of all ages and abilities. The greatest gift of the Orff-Schulwerk approach is awakening children's senses and engaging them in a total awareness of music. Orff also believed that musical experiences must begin early, during the first year of life. He believed that every child is educable and that unmusical children are very rare.

Moving, speaking, singing, improvising, playing instruments, and listening are all important activities in the Orff work for young children. In Orff classes, children are actively involved together;

they are motivated to participate in making music. Through these experiences, they learn musical concepts and build musical skills.

Folk music is important in Orff-Schulwerk activity because folk music is created from the language and culture of its people.

> One of the basic premises of the Schulwerk is that each culture should begin with its own speech and song heritage, rhymes, proverbs, children's chants, games, and songs. In some cultures these may be based on rhythm and melody patterns quite different from the original German models. (Shamrock, 1986)

The role of the teacher in the Orff music class is to look objectively at his or her own heritage and draw materials from his or her own culture. The teachers are the ones who plan the activities, provide the instruments, and act as helpers. They should be creative, dare to try different approaches to achieve better results, and guide the children in their music-making activities.

Main Goals
1. To use speech and movement as the springboard for musical experiences.
2. To give an immediacy of enjoyment and meaning to the child through active participation.
3. To encourage the feeling that speech, movement, play, and song are one.
4. To give a completely physical, nonintellectual background in rhythm and melody, thus laying a foundation of experience necessary to the later understanding of music and of musical notation.
5. To cultivate musical improvisation, invention, and development of musical creativity.

Materials Relating to Orff and Early Childhood

Beginning with the very first volume of *Music for Children* (1957) materials for early childhood have been a part of the Schulwerk. This volume contains some limited range songs, simple body percussion pieces, and instrumentarium arrangements that could be adapted for young children.

In 1982, a preschool edition of *Music for Children*, the American Edition was published. This edition of the Schulwerk is full of traditional American songs, chants, and games as well as pictures of children in action. At the end of the book are articles on movement, speech and song, improvisation, instrumental work, listening, rhymes and poetry, and involving parents by prominent early childhood Orff educators.

Another approach to early childhood music education using the Orff philosophy is *Kids Make Music, Babies Make Music Too!* by Lynn Kleiner. In this book she provides suggestions for songs, chants, movement activities, and instrument playing for young children. The book contains a mixture of traditional and composed repertoire and is only one of many materials, including videos, that are available by this author.

A wonderful video showing Orff in action with preschool children was made in 1982 by Richard Gill, Helen Newton, and Michael Atherton and is available from the American Orff-Schulwerk Association in Cleveland, Ohio. The video is entitled *I Can Make Music* and shows children moving freely to music, playing found-sound musical instruments and drums, and listening to music.

In Conclusion

Orff-Schulwerk is a teaching and learning approach, not a method. Its approach to music education for the child begins with the premise that feeling precedes intellectual understanding. Carl Orff started with the basic element of music that is most natural to the child: rhythm. It is through the rhythm of the child's speech and movement that we can best encourage him or her to understand music. In addition, children need a balance between emotional and intellectual stimulation to develop as healthy human beings. Orff-Schulwerk provides this balance through active involvement in music making.

References

Keetman, Gunild. 1970. *Elementaria*. London: Schott.

Kleiner, Lynn. 1998. *Kids make music, babies make music too!* Manhattan Beach: Music Rhapsody.

Orff, Carl and Keetman, Gunild. 1957. Edited by Margaret Murray. *Music for children*. London: Schott.

Orff, Carl. 1978. *Carl Orff: The Schulwerk*. New York: Schott.

Regner, Hermann, Coordinator. 1982. *Music for Children* Vol. 1, *Orff-Schulwerk,* American Edition. New York: Schott.

Shamrock, Mary. 1986. Orff-Schulwerk: An integrated foundation. *Music Educators Journal*, 72 (6): 51–55.

Warner, Brigitte. 1991. *Orff-Schulwerk: Applications for the classroom*. Englewood Cliffs: Prentice-Hall, Inc.

Chet-Yeng Loong is an assistant professor at Baldwin-Wallace College in Berea, Ohio. This article originally appeared in the April 2000 issue of Ohio's Triad. Reprinted by permission.

No Known Destination: Pre-Primary Music and Reggio Emilia
by Carol L. Matthews

When asked to be the music teacher for the new pre-primary program for three- and four-year-olds based on the Reggio Emilia approach to early childhood education at Foothills School for Arts and Sciences, I accepted readily, believing that I was fully prepared. After all, my doctorate is in music, I had piloted early childhood music programs at Boise State and the Children's School just last year, and had done research and study with the Music Education faculty at Boise State.

I was ready. Or so I believed. What I didn't know was that I had just stepped into territory with the wrong map and no known destination.

Reggio Emilia is an approach to education developed by parents and teachers in the cities of those names in northern Italy in 1945, immediately after the war. They wanted something very different. Reading from some of the reform educators of the 1930s, specifically John Dewey, they created pre-primary, even infant schools, where the children would direct the direction of inquiry. Teachers problematize, bringing questions to the children, and then the children begin the inquiry—what are shadows? How are they made? What makes them go away? Teachers bring questions to the children but the children find the answers and while they look for the answers, their journeys are documented. They draw, paint, color the things they see and do. Photographs are used to record their work. The conversations they have are transcribed and the things they write down as they become literate are documented. All of these things are used to decorate the walls of their room as well as hallways, porches, bathroom, all the places of the space that they are in. Parents are a vital part to the process and one morning each week is spent by parents with the teachers in the classroom looking at and discussing the activities of the week, what the children have done and how they have done it, what has changed, where they are going, what the parents see as ways in which to facilitate the inquires, how they and/or the teachers can extend promising activities.

Attending the meetings of parents and the initiating faculty, I was attracted by the title of the Reggio Emilia handbook, an anthology of articles and interviews, *The Hundred Languages of Children* (Edward, Gandini, Forman, 1993). Though nothing in the book and the articles I read spoke directly to a music program per se, I liked the idea of music being a form of expression for small children, one of their languages of development and learning. I had a whole lot of songs, chants, activities, learning strategies that I felt would help the children learn to be expressive. I could really teach them music. However, my program that had worked so well everywhere else fell apart in the first week.

I knew going into the program that Reggio Emilia was what we sometimes refer to as child-directed, and I had a few twinges about that. How is it possible to teach the very complex language of music if the child is the one that decides where we are to go? But, oh well, maybe that was OK for language arts, construction, visual arts, but with music we could work a little at a time in structured activities, surely, with clearly defined goals.

Well, the children were wonderful. They listened to the first song, sang with me on the second song, then started drifting away. "Wait a minute," I said, "don't you want to hear about…?" "No," was their inevitable reply, "I want to do…" whatever was on their mind to do. By the end of the week I realized that all my prepared lessons, songs, and activities were only that, materials that had little or nothing to do with what was going on in their very busy little lives. What to do?

Seeing my confusion, the principal teachers, Anne Cirillo and Shirley Rau, were quick to reassure me. "They love to sing," they told me, "they love to have you in the room." So I continued to come and I would start each session with a song, just one, that the children could sing with me while in their opening circle.

Sometimes I would introduce an instrument to the children, one that they could try out, such as a guitar or my old student violin. But after the opening activities I frequently found myself assisting with other things—dramatic play, draw-

ing, reading, or creating signs—rarely doing anything musical. After the initial "messing around" period the instruments, too, seemed to be ignored. While these things were fine as far as they went, I felt I wasn't doing anything special and certainly not contributing to a musical language of expression for the children. I felt adrift and without direction, my careful routines nonworkable, and very anxious about proceeding without my usual road map.

I returned to the books and articles about Reggio that had been given to me. There was nothing about music. (Interestingly, there was also almost nothing on the Internet. Though teachers at other centers expressed frustration with integrating music, few had come up with any workable solutions.) Music was mentioned as a language of expression even in the original centers in Reggio Emilia in Italy, but no where did it say, as it did about visual and language arts, how it was integrated into the classroom. As I reread the material about Reggio I watched our "atelierista," our art teacher, Melanie Fales, work with the children, and I began to realize that there needed to be another way to approach the making of music in this classroom. I had to change my own thinking about how to conceptualize the acquisition of music, especially when considering it as a language. Turning things around, I began to ask myself questions about how the student could *be* musical rather than become musical. How were they already musical and how could I foster that?

Melanie provided tools for the children to be artistic, to create art works: crayons, paints of all types, pastels, clay, colored and noncolored pencils, etc. Could I also provide tools with which they could experiment musically? As we observed the children working with visual arts, we realized that "messing around" wasn't a bad thing; indeed, it seemed to be a necessary activity for the children to do before they could manipulate the materials more carefully.

Had I been too quick to see "messing around" as non-musical? And what about documentation? How could I document, as Melanie did, the sounds and musical activities of the students so that parents and teachers could use and build upon them?

The first question, providing the students with musical tools, was both easy and difficult to solve. I had a small budget. I could buy some instruments for the students to work with. But there's a problem with instruments. They make noise. In some cases, a lot of noise. Some children seem to enjoy making the loudest noises they can.

We found this out when I brought some small accordions to class. The noise of just two or three children playing these instruments in a standard-sized classroom was distressing not just to the other students but to the other teachers as well! All other activity seemed to stop as my little group experimented. So loud instruments were out. Instead I selected instruments that the children could play both individually and share, while not intruding too greatly on the rest of the class: brightly colored, small child-sized maracas, a plastic, see-through rain stick with brightly colored beads inside (a parent quickly then donated a real rain stick, the same size as the plastic one), bell clusters, a slit drum with mallets, a plastic slide whistle. The violin and guitar became a permanent part of the music center as did kazoos and harmonicas (one for each child).

Now our opening circle was not just choral, but orchestral, with everyone both singing and playing. And messing around became a part of every session I initiated. The instruments became part of dance sessions, dramatic play activity, animal exploration. As the students integrated the instruments into other activities, their use of them became more focused, more controlled, and more expressive.

Documentation, however, presented greater problems. The obvious way to document any musical activity, of course, is to audio record it. We had several small, hand-held tape recorders in the classroom and at my request all the teachers began to record whatever musical activities happened to occur. But what to do with it after that?

Taking the tapes home and listening to them, I decided that the songs the children were making up needed to be transcribed. This was less time consuming than I at first feared. There were only a few real songs (with a lot of messing around) and the songs sometimes had words and sometimes didn't. I began keeping a notebook then, of actual songs which could then be photocopied. While taping the children singing (usually while they were doing other activities), the other teachers would try to write down the words as part of their regular documentation of student expression, giving me a real shortcut in trying to decipher what was on the tape. I then saved the more lucent recordings, dubbing them on a separate tape, which I could then play for the parents and teachers at the end of the week, showing them the notebook of collected musical expression. This, in turn, has led to the parents and teachers understanding far more directly just how musical the children are, the variety of ways in which children are musical, and the endless possibilities there are to extend musical activity.

For me this is just the beginning of a new way to explore music possibilities for three- and four-year-olds. Already I am seeing many, many different directions for the students to be musical. It is at times difficult, frustrating, and dismaying not to have an itinerary of specific long term goals, learning objectives and behaviors that are such a part of the education process. I still struggle with the idea that if I don't know where I am going, how can I know what to bring to each session? The only answer is trust. We must trust the students to take the tools we give them, to create the landmarks, read the signs, and move them and us to new levels of expression and understanding.

Carol L. Matthews is adjunct instructor of music education, theory, and ear training at Boise State University and full-time music instructor at Foothills School for Arts and Sciences in Boise, Idaho. This article originally appeared in the Winter 1999 issue of Idaho Music Notes. *Reprinted by permission.*

Developing Musicianship through Musical Play
by Cynthia Crump Taggart

Edwin Gordon's theories about how children learn music and the practice that naturally flows out of those theories are rooted in the belief that children learn music through processes that are similar to those used in learning language. Consider the following. Children learn language by being immersed in a culture that is rich in language. No one directly teaches children to understand language or to speak it; they learn to do so in an informal way, and their ability to learn and use language depends upon the quality of their language environments and natural propensities.

Children hear language being spoken all around them; sometimes it is spoken directly to them, and other times they experience it through overhearing conversations. Eventually, children begin to "play with" the sounds in the language through language babble.

Throughout this time, children are developing a listening vocabulary that has not yet found its way into their speech, for children can understand a great deal more than they can actually say. Babble eventually gives way to the imitation of words, with and without the understanding of the meaning of those words, and finally to children speaking words, phrases, and whole sentences with meaning. When children enter formal language instruction, they will learn to read and write what they can already understand and speak. Further along in their language development, they will learn to label the parts of the language with which they are already functionally proficient.

Now consider the musical parallels. Children need to be immersed in a rich music environment in order to develop a listening vocabulary in music and subsequently to begin to "play with" the sounds of music. Eventually, children will develop an imitative speaking vocabulary in music, with the ultimate goal of early childhood music instruction being children's audiation of music, which is giving meaning to the music that they hear and perform in terms of tonality and meter. In the same way that children teach themselves language syntax, they teach themselves music syntax.

This syntax enables them to function within tonalities or meters in a logical, meaningful way so that they can predict what might come next in music. Only when children can audiate can they create music that has meaning in terms of the musical syntax of adult culture. After they have developed this sense of music syntax and can use it to understand what they hear and perform, they have the readiness for formal music instruction. Only at this point should parents consider instruction in the reading and writing of music for their children. Eventually, in formal music instruction, children can learn to label the parts of what they can already understand, perform, read, and write.

Gordon (1997, p. 33) has described developmental types and stages of preparatory audiation through which all children progress musically. Although general age ranges are included in figure 1, these are estimates at best. A child's musical age is not tied to his or her chronological age; there are some adults who are still in musical acculturation. The types and stages of preparatory audiation are described in detail in *A Music Learning Theory for Newborn and Young Children* (Gordon, p. 38).

When a child is in preparatory audiation, informal guidance rather than formal instruction in music is appropriate. The type and stage of preparatory audiation in which a child is engaged, tonally or rhythmically, helps to determine what form that musical guidance should take.

Teachers quickly become aware that children's tonal and rhythm development do not necessarily parallel one another. In fact, most children are stronger in one dimension than the other and progress more rapidly in that dimension than in the other. A child's strength in one or the other dimension will be related to his or her degree of tonal or rhythm aptitude (potential to achieve tonally or rhythmically) in combination with the quality of his or her musical environment as it relates to each dimension.

The development of music aptitude in young children is one of the reasons that Gordon is so adamant about the importance of an appropriate music environment for young children. Music aptitudes are developmental, meaning that they are affected by the environment when children are young. The better the quality of the music environment for a young child, the more potential that child will have for learning music throughout life. This places a tremendous responsibility on parents and early childhood music teachers to offer the best possible music environment for each and every child.

Practical Applications
If parents wish their children to be as fluent in music as they are in language, they must strive to

create a music environment for their children that is as rich as their children's language environment. Unfortunately, this is difficult and sometimes impossible, for although all parents, barring disability, can speak with fluency to and for their children, many parents are unable to sing in tune and with musicianship and move freely.

As a result, the musical models for many children are inadequate to support the development of their potentials in music. Fortunately, many parents seek outside help in creating music-rich environments for their children, but what should be the staples in such environments?

Informal, Developmentally Appropriate Environment

Children from the very beginnings of their lives must be immersed in music environments with no expectation toward correctness and with the opportunity to interact in those environments in whatever way they feel comfortable. They must be surrounded by singing and movement and allowed to listen, watch, and musically explore as they wish. Some children may pay rapt attention whereas others may wander and not even make eye contact. Some children may cling to their parents while others may wander about the room or engage fully in class activities.

Although, seemingly off-task behavior may be frustrating to a teacher or parent, such behavior is developmentally appropriate and should be allowed to occur. Adults cannot make accurate judgments concerning how much a child is absorbing musically by watching his or her apparent focus on the task. A child who appears to be aimlessly wandering can be learning as much as a child who seems to be actively engaged.

All responses from children should be encouraged. When a child responds musically, the adult who is guiding the musical activity should imitate the response and, whenever possible, incorporate that response into the classroom music making.

For example, if, in a moment of silence after the teacher performs a song or chant, a child were to chant a rhythm pattern of his or her own, the teacher should echo the child's pattern and then improvise a change incorporating the child's pattern. In this way, the guidance is child- rather than teacher-directed.

Only if children are encouraged to explore the musical sounds of their environment through informal music making will they eventually become assimilated into "adult" musical culture. Children must be immersed in a playful music environment in which their music utterances are nurtured and treasured.

Developing a Repertoire of Songs and Chants

In order to develop a listening vocabulary, children must have the opportunity to hear a large repertoire of songs and chants in a wide variety of

TYPE	STAGE
ACCULTURATION: Birth; age 2–4: participates with little consciousness of the environment.	1. **ABSORPTION:** hears and aurally collects the sounds of the environment. 2. **RANDOM RESPONSE:** moves and babbles in response to, but without relations to, the sounds of music in the environment. 3. **PURPOSEFUL RESPONSE:** tries to relate movement and babble to the sounds of music in the environment.
IMITATION: Ages 2–4 to 3–5: participates with conscious thought focused primarily on the environment.	4. **SHEDDING EGOCENTRICITY:** recognizes that a movement and babble do not match the sounds of music in the environment. 5. **BREAKING THE CODE:** imitates with some precision the sounds of music in the environment, specifically tonal patterns and rhythm patterns.
ASSIMILATION: Ages 3–5 to age 4–6: participates with conscious thought focused primarily on self.	6. **INTROSPECTION:** recognizes the lack of coordination between singing, changing, breathing, and movement. 7. **COORDINATION:** coordinates singing and chanting with breathing and movement.

Figure 1. Types and stages of preparatory audiation

tonalities and meters. These songs and chants, combined with movement, provide the foundation upon which a child can begin to develop his or her musical vocabularies. It is from these songs and chants that children begin to develop a sense of the context of music. Children should not be expected to sing with the adult who is performing the song repertoire; rather, the songs and chants should be performed for the children, who in time will explore parts of the songs musically through babble.

In a culture whose music is primarily in duple meter and major tonality, why should children be exposed to less-frequently-heard tonalities and meters? Children learn what something is by learning what it is not. In other words, children will have a much deeper understanding of duple meter when they have other meters to compare to duple. Only when they have experienced triple meter and meters that are typically notated in fives and sevens can children really understand what is special about duple, because what is special about duple is what differentiates it from other meters.

In the same way, what is special about major is what differentiates it from other tonalities. Therefore, children need to hear a wide variety of tonalities and meters, not so that they become fluent in locrian, for example, but so that they can function within major with greater understanding. Although singing songs in unusual tonalities and meters may be difficult for adults who are carrying a lifetime of "major, duple baggage," children find other tonalities and meters extremely compelling and no more complex than major and duple.

Songs and chants should be performed mostly without and occasionally with text. Because children's language environments tend to be better in terms of quality and quantity than most music environments, the texts of songs tend to be more accessible to children than the tonal and rhythm contents of the songs.

As a result, the children tend to focus on the text at the expense of the songs' tonal and rhythm contents, interfering with music learning. To counteract this, in early childhood settings, songs and chants should be performed primarily without text. Text can be added later when the children have already had sufficient immersion in the tonal and rhythmic elements of the song or chant.

Developing a Repertoire of Movements
Movement is readiness for stylistic, rhythmic, and, to some extent, even tonal understanding in music (Gordon, 1997; Moog, 1976; Valerio, Reynolds,

Bolton, Taggart, Gordon, 1998). As a result, children should have extensive opportunities to develop comfort with a large repertoire of movement. Gordon (1997) believes that the best way to develop coordinated movement is through the systematic incorporation of Laban's effort elements—flow, weight, space, and time. Laban, (1971) believed that every movement represents a combination of the movement elements flow, weight, space, and time, and that each element can be represented by a continuum.

The ends of the flow continuum are free and bound, the ends of the weight continuum are strong and gentle, the ends of the space continuum are direct and indirect, and the ends of the time continuums are fast and slow. Children should gain comfort with movements at both ends of each continuum, beginning with flow, followed by weight, space, and time.

Children need to learn to coordinate their bodies through such movement early on so that they can use this body awareness to enhance their music understanding. Reynolds (1995) found that children as young as 10 months old are able to imitate continuous, flowing movements and that children who are expressive in their musical performances have demonstrated their ability to flow in movement.

Continuous, flowing movements appear to be fundamental to the development of movement skills and musicianship in children and should be modeled and encouraged extensively while performing music for young children, whereas movement to beat appears to be of secondary importance.

Developing a Repertoire of Tonal and Rhythmic Patterns
In the same way that children must develop a vocabulary of words in language, they must develop a vocabulary of tonal and rhythm patterns in music. They will use this vocabulary to understand the music that they hear and perform and to create music of their own in the same way that people use familiar words in language to articulate their own ideas. This vocabulary is developed through tonal and rhythm pattern instruction. In addition to facilitating music vocabulary development, pattern instruction is important in that it gives teachers an opportunity to interact with each child individually and to adapt instruction to the needs of the individual child.

For example, a child who is already successfully imitating patterns will have different tonal needs than a child who has yet to make a tonal utterance. During pattern instruction, the teacher can give the two children different types of guidance. Tonal patterns are always performed after a song in the same tonality and key and rhythm patterns are always performed after a song or chant in the same meter and tempo. In this way, the patterns are given context.

Conclusions

Gordon's early childhood music methodology flows naturally from his theories about how children learn music. The primary focus of instruction, according to Gordon, should be the development of tonal and rhythm audiation, or a sense of tonal and rhythm syntax, in children so that they can bring tonal and rhythmic understanding to the music that they hear and perform. This occurs by immersing children in playful environments that are rich in singing, chanting, tonalities, meters, and movement. In a developmentally appropriate environment, children are given the opportunities to play with music with the guidance of teachers who are sensitive to their developmental needs.

References

Gordon, E. E. (1997). *A music learning theory for newborn and young children*. Chicago: G.I.A.

Laban, R. (1971). *The mastery of movement*. London: London MacDonald and Evans.

Moog, H. (1976). *The musical experience of the pre-school child*. Translated by Claudia Clarke. London: Schott and Co.

Reynolds, A. M. (1995). An investigation of the movement responses performed by children 18 months to 3 years of age and their care givers to rhythm chants in duple and triple meters. *Dissertation Abstracts International, 56* (04), 1283. (University Microfilms No. AAC9527531)

Valerio, W. H., Reynolds, A. M., Bolton, B. M., Taggart, C. C., and Gordon, E. E. 1981. *Music play*. Chicago: G.I.A.

Cynthia Crump Taggart is an associate professor of music education and director of the early childhood music program at Michigan State University in East Lansing. This article originally appeared in the May/June 2000 issue of Ohio's Triad. *Reprinted by permission.*

An Interview with Phyllis Weikart
by Linda Weyman

You have done extensive research and study on early childhood education. In your opinion, what is the most important thing that we can do to enable our children to be successful?

Weikart: I have to answer "steady beat" because we know that children who have steady beat independence seem to develop increased comprehension capability, clearer enunciation and speech flow. Increased attending as well as personal coordination and in-tune singing. Another answer to this is music and movement every day in school.

What activities do you suggest that we emphasize with our students?

Weikart: Obviously steady beat activities, including rocking. Activities that build the visual and aural attending ability. Activities that develop pitch relationships for in-tune singing (we use a body scale). Activities to build coordination ability.

When should we begin these activities and until what age?

Weikart: These activities should begin with three and four year olds, and continue through the elementary years. The body scale should be introduced in late first grade. Rhythm should be introduced in second grade. Stay in steady beat before that.

You are recognized as an expert in movement. Why is movement important for all of us?

Weikart: Movement uses all levels of the brain and integrates right and left hemispheres for all students. Purposeful movement is used throughout life.

Please tell us about your research on beat awareness and its impact on academic success.

Weikart: I have been studying steady beat since 1980. We have found links to reading, vocabulary, and math comprehension. Our latest research is answered in question #1. Between 1981 and 1991, the percentage of teenagers with steady beat dropped in half. The females in 1981 showed over 80% of them successful and in 1991, only 48% were successful. The males dropped from 66% to 30%. My daughter tested two 2nd grade classes last fall and found only 2 children who were competent with steady beat. This was out of 27 and 25 students in the classes. I myself find fewer than 10% of kindergarten children competent. We are testing preschool children this fall.

You have traveled to many different countries conducting research and providing workshops. What difference and what similarities have you found among people, especially the children?

Weikart: We have international teenagers here for a four-week program each summer. They are always better overall than the American teens. English is the only "untimed" language. This affects our children. Other languages have regularity of accent. Because so many of our children are given rhythm of the words, their comprehension is fractured.

You have been described as a "master" of sequence and process teaching. Can you explain the importance of correct sequence and process for teaching and learning?

Weikart: To me, it is obvious that one needs to be aware of the simple-to-more complex sequencing and not "pick apples" off the tree. I don't believe students have been schooled in sequence in our undergraduate and graduate training. Today, many children do not come to us with the basic foundation in place. We need to build the foundation by knowing what are the steps. Concerning process, a consistent process is essential for learners. I have developed the movement-based active learning process that can be used with any curriculum.

Do your sequential and process teaching methods correlate with current brain research concerning the way people learn new information? Is this true for all ages, not just children?

Weikart: People who have been involved say, "YES!" I had Carla Hannaford from "Smart Moves" in a workshop that I did. She was most impressed with how it all fits together. The sequence and process are needed throughout life. A beginner is a beginner at any age. Just because we are 15 or 30, or 60, doesn't mean that we don't need sequence and process.

What other fields of research is your "High/Scope Foundation" currently involved with?

Weikart: The High/Scope Educational Research Foundation of which my "Education through Movement: Building the Foundation" is an Associate Division, is best known for its work in Early Childhood. They have been involved with Early Childhood research since 1963. High/Scope has the longest ongoing longitudinal research on the effects of early childhood education in the world. Children who are not given choices from the early years and on up, don't fare as well in life as children who are given choices.

Is there anything else that you would like to share with us?

Weikart: I have worked with teenagers for 37 consecutive summers and I am saddened about the abilities of young people in the last 10 years vs. 20 and 30 years ago. This is the same age population every summer, but the bottom has fallen out. When I do rhythm exercises and folk dances with them, I start where I would start with 1st and 2nd graders, but I make it age appropriate. I so want any person with whom I come in contact with to be successful. I work to that end. Everyone should feel good when they have opportunities to be involved with movement and music.

Linda Weyman teaches music at Sacred Hearts Academy in Honolulu, Hawaii. This is an excerpt from an article that originally appeared in the September 1999 issue of Hawaii's Leka Nu Hou. *Reprinted by permission.*

Section 2

 # Lesson Ideas

The activities mentioned in this section have been used with success. They may be implemented in various settings and will provide a fun path to musical understanding for young learners.

 Section 2

Lesson Ideas

Spatial, Personal, and Relational Language Concept Implications for the General Music Classroom
by Betty Ellis

Do you ever find your kindergartners roaming aimlessly in circle formations? How about lines of children that look more like squiggles? Do you ever struggle with the child who thinks all the turns should be theirs, all the instruments should be theirs and they haven't had a turn unless they have played *all* the instruments or played *all* the parts in the story?

From a teaching perspective, it may help to consider the ages at which the average child acquires spatial, personal and relational concepts. With the increasing number of special needs children in all of our K–6 classes and with inclusion on the rise, this information must be adapted since "average" must be adjusted to meet the needs of the children we teach.

Children learn the concept of self (I, my, mine, me) between the ages of 2.0 to 2.6 years; the concept of others (he, she, her, him) between the ages of 2.6 to 3 years; the concept of you at 3.0 to 3.6 years, and the concept of community (we, our) between the ages of 4.6 to 5.6 years. If you have a child who is not able to share or take turns, it may be that the child is selfish and self-centered. On the other hand, it may be that the child is delayed in the development of the skills and concepts relating to person. As a teacher, you must constantly reinforce the concept in the vocabulary that you choose in speaking to the children. Provide many experiences for sharing. Describe, using children's names, who has the instrument, who will share it next and how that sharing is to take place. Don't assume that the children will figure it out. Many won't. You may have to take the time between turns to redirect partners by name, close proximity and physical contact in the actual trading of instruments. Once the children have

traded successfully, reinforce the concept by trading again before leaving the activity frame. Transfer of knowledge will only happen after successful repetition within the same activity.

To move with walking steps in locomotor motion, one student following another (walking in a line) requires spatial relationship concepts. Children acquire the concepts of in front of, in back of, and next to between the ages of 3.6 to 4.0 years. However, they don't acquire the concepts of beside until 4.0 to 4.6 years and the concepts of behind, ahead of, first, and last until 5.0 to 5.6 years. If a child is not successful when directed to get behind another student, you may want to redirect by saying in back of, while patting your own back for visual modeling. Then reinforce the concept by saying, "Susy is behind Adam." An alternate instruction for the child having difficulty understanding beside would be to use the phrase next to. In each instance, reinforcing the concept with statement like, "Sam is standing beside Tom," will help all children acquire the concepts needed for success.

For children who are visual learners, I made a model of a footpath the children follow when choosing instruments. I used the die-cuts in the teacher workroom, made matching left and right feet in several different colors, glued them to black construction paper in sequential walking order, laminated the whole thing and duck-taped it to the floor of the music room. Now my preschoolers and kindergartners practice making a line on their way to pick up their instrument. It saves time, lots of chaos and reinforces spatial concepts.

Moving in a circular pattern is certainly a much harder expectation and it's more than centrifugal force! A wise teacher once gave me the hint to have the children focus on the shoulder of the person in front of them, which raises their line of sight off the floor while giving a visual reference. I have also put dotted lines of duck tape in a circle pattern on the floor as a reference for the children. Some children are more successful at maintaining a moving circular line if they can see the entire visual reference. I have found that moving without holding hands is much easier for younger children to maintain successfully than the hand holding. If you do choose hand holding, make sure to provide opportunities to let go of hands at some point (cadences, section endings) with careful planning (clap hands, turn around, touch the floor) built into the music to relieve the stress of holding another person's hand.

Many of the challenges we face as teachers of music are not caused by the music, but by misunderstanding the development of children. Constant diagnosis, assessment and detailed planning will increase the appropriate developmental understanding of our children, with their specific abilities and disabilities, so crucial to a successful music program.

Betty Ellis teaches preschool through sixth grade general music in the Anchorage School District in Alaska. This article originally appeared in the Winter 1999 issue of the Alaska Music Educator. *Reprinted by permission.*

Musical Playtime for Developing Young Minds
by Debbie Fahmie

After taking a course in brain development of young children this past summer, I became intrigued by the subject. The more I learned about how young children's brains function and develop, the more aware I became of how vital appropriate music and movement activities are in the process. I realized that many of the musical activities that are so important in the development of children need to occur before we ever see them in Kindergarten. Once the primary aged child does reach Kindergarten, they certainly need to engage in these types of activities more regularly than their scheduled music classes allow. I felt committed to reach beyond my own music classroom. So, my passion became an outreach to the preschool and primary teacher.

Here are a few facts that might help you to understand the importance of reaching out to primary teachers to help them feel comfortable in providing some of the music and movement activities that are essential in developing a whole child.

- A child's brain develops most rapidly from birth to age 4.
- Fifty percent of a child's intelligence is acquired by age 4; 80 percent by age 8.
- By age 5, a child's personality, self-concept, emotional development and character will be almost complete. (Primary source: Special Report "How a Child's Brain develops," Feb. 3, 1997 issue, *Time* magazine.)

As music specialists, we are all aware of the impact music education has on a child's learning and social development. If such a crucial window of learning occurs in the very young child, how important is it that we take a role in helping to provide quality, age-appropriate opportunities for these children?

As I began to connect with our preschool and Kindergarten programs in my county, I found that many of the most well-intentioned teachers were not comfortable with their own musical skills and therefore resorted to very commercial types of musical materials for their students. The materials being used were not only inappropriate for young voices, but did nothing to engage in the development of the whole child. We cannot expect the administrators or the classroom teachers to be knowledgeable about making better choices (entertainment vs. learning). They really need our expertise to guide them. By passing along the philosophies of experts such as John Feierabend, we can help these teachers make better choices.

The outreach in my county involved workshops for the preschool staff members with whom I shared resources, philosophies and, most importantly, modeled the processes that I was recommending they use on a regular basis with all children. Processes included singing, moving, instrument playing, language development, creation, exploration and discovery.

In order for developmental musical play to be successful, the classroom must be structured in such a way as to allow for child-initiated, child-directed, and teacher-supported experiences to occur. Many suggested activities became very doable to teachers once they were modeled in a workshop. In order for meaningful learning to take place, children need repetition, routine and engagement. When musical play is structured with these three elements, children will be empowered to make connections. The best brains are those that are in symmetry (whole brained). Music engages both of the hemispheres. The following suggestions were made to help lead primary classroom teachers through enjoyable and successful experiences and to feel prepared to sing, dance, play, and create with their students!

Singing

Sing to and with your students often. Sing your dialogue (use just 2 or 3 pitches). Turn daily routines, such as role call, into a musical and playful experience.

Space and Movement

Allow your children to have many experiences in manipulating their space. Play the "Bubble Game" often. This game allows children to remain in control of their bodies while exploring creative movement. It helps them to understand and experience pathways. Work on personal and shared space in this game as well. Use carpet squares to identify space. When playing instruments, children want to have a turn at all the instruments. This can be very time consuming. The carpet squares can become the "home" for the instrument, helping the students to move to a new instrument quickly. Establish this routine and practice it often. Mirroring activities are great for focusing the students. Sometimes we forget how good it feels to put on some beautiful music and warm up our bodies with stretches. Children love to do this as well. This is a great way to slip in some wonderful classical music. When selecting music for warm-ups as well as mirroring activities, be sure to use instrumental music so that the words of the song don't get in the way of the directions that you are giving or showing the child. Three things that we all need to increase our brain capacity are 1) water, 2) air, and 3) exercise. Be sure that some quality, deep breathing exercises are part of your warm-up.

Instrument Playing

Quite often I hear classroom teachers say that they don't use instruments because the children get out of control and the management of the instruments takes up too much time. Here I went into great detail to share some classroom management techniques to encourage the use of rhythm band instruments. While sharing your best practices, be sure to share even the simplest ideas that help the efficient and successful distribution, use and collection of instruments with the classroom teacher.

We have found in our county that many instruments have come out of the closets for the first time and that requests are being made for additional instruments to be purchased for the preschool and kinder classes. Again, stay involved and make knowledgeable recommendations on what should be ordered.

Language

Experiences in language are the beginning of a journey into literacy. Allow children to "play" with the language of the songs you sing. Encourage your students to create variations or rewrite the words to a song. Use poetry and nursery rhymes to create with.

Creation

Creation is one of the ultimate goals of many activities. Many times we start with a song, learn it, play with it, change it and finally use it as the foundation for our own creation. It is very important to teach children to do this. That's why it is unacceptable to buy a CD and allow the students to do nothing more than learn the words and sing along with it.

Preschool children thrive on repetition. That is a definite benefit to you as a teacher. By popular demand, you must do your classes' favorite songs over and over again. There is no way that you can maintain a high level of excitement with a song that you've sung for the umpteenth time this week unless you take advantage of using that song as a springboard into creation.

As soon as the students are comfortable with a song, begin to make that song blossom, as your classes' own creation. Think of new ways to perform the song. Add movement. Add sign language or gestures. Add instruments. Act it out. Be dramatic with it. Turn it into a game—a circle game, then a partner game. Change the words. Change the meaning (for example "The Bear Went Over the Mountain" changes to "The Bear Went to the Mall").

The teacher needs to model all of these ideas, but then needs to turn the creation over to the students. Allow them to come up with the variations. Have the idea person demonstrate and then have the entire class try it out. This teaches creativity and productivity to the child. It also helps the teacher identify who her idea people are; who her problem solvers are; who her leaders are. This is a great way for a teacher to discover hidden talents within their students.

Remember that the brain works in wavelengths. Each part of the creation is like a building block—however, there needs to be downtime built into the activity. Spread your ideas out over days. Again, the children love the repetition and will ask for the song the next day anyway. If you present too many ideas within one session, the brain will not optimize all the benefits. Downtime allows neural connections to solidify.

Exploration and Discovery

Exploration and discovery are vital to a child's life experiences. In addition to teacher directed exploration and discovery, children need the opportunity to play with sound on their own, without perimeters set by a teacher. A Sound Center set up in your classroom can present your students with valuable opportunities to work with sound and to become sensitive to the properties of sound, music and composition.

I hope that this article will encourage you to reach out to your primary classroom teachers and empower them to engage in musical play with their students. Carl Orff said, "The work of children is play." The rewards of your efforts will be far reaching. One of our preschool teachers wrote, "The children love the songs and activities that you shared with us. We've used several of them with our Good Samaritan Senior Buddies during our bi-weekly visits...80-year-olds enjoy the songs just as much as the 4-year-olds."

Debbie Fahmie teaches chorus, Orff Ensemble, and general music at Cypress Elementary School in Kissimmee, Florida. This article originally appeared in the May 2000 issue of the Florida Music Director. *Reprinted by permission.*

Music and Movement for Infants and Toddlers: Naturally Wonder-full
by John M. Feierabend

Musical behavior is basic to all cultures, both primitive and sophisticated. And yet, 20th-century gains in music knowledge and technology have been accompanied by the decline of music traditions and behaviors that once were a part of every child's heritage.

Today, as in the past, *singing, movement* and *listening* behaviors enhance everyday life. *Singing:* We soothe infants with lullabies, join in familiar melodies such as "Happy Birthday," or raise our voices in song during worship. *Movement:* we rock the infant to the beat of the music, clap in rhythm to cheering at a sports event, and dance to music at a wedding reception. *Listening:* we attend school concerts, select and listen to recordings, and respond to the nuances of concert music performed by professional orchestras and choral groups.

Competence and comfort with basic musical behaviors usually lead to increased pleasure and satisfaction. By developing children's innate musical potential from birth throughout childhood we contribute to life-long enjoyment of the rewards of music. Basic musical behaviors include the following:

1. in-tune and expressive singing;
2. moving in rhythm with music;
3. listening with sensitivity to the musical and expressive qualities of the music.

Expressive sensitivity, though hard to define, is critical for understanding music. In *The Republic*, Plato speaks about music as an art form with the potential to deliver a message "below the surface."

A fine composer uses the tools of music to create works that convey something "below the surface." Insightful performers realize the composer's communicative intent as they recreate the music. The process is completed when attentive and perceptive listeners hear and respond mentally and emotionally to the music. If, however, the listeners lack the expressive sensitivity necessary to perceive the "message below the surface," the message falls on deaf ears.

Sensitivity to the expressive qualities in music must be nurtured during the earliest months of life. We must sing to our babies, dance with our babies, and use quality children's music literature when doing so. Later, when these children become adults, their musical sensitivity will allow them to offer their children a nurturing musical environment.

A century ago, many families instinctively engaged their very young children in activities that were ideal for developing musicality: singing traditional children's songs, making music, listening to music, and moving to music. There was little need for courses in early childhood music or for classes attended by infants and toddlers with their parents.

Today, a consumer-directed technology delivers quantities of musical junk food to children. This commercialized music, though pervasive, lacks the musical nutrition that all children need. Recent and current research has awakened music educators' interest in music and movement experiences during early childhood, and a variety of evidence underlines the need for rich musical experiences throughout the early childhood years. Long before formal research data became available, however, many parents shared well-remembered traditional musical activities with their infants and toddlers. These activities and experiences nurtured the child's developing neural network and fostered growth in musical coordination, comprehension, and sensitivity.

I have conducted interviews with many senior citizens, asking them to recall a song, rhyme, or game that could be played with a baby on their lap.[1] The elderly—those over 80 years in age—recollected and offered a broader and more diverse repertoire than those 60–80 years in age. Adults between the ages of 40–60 years had a very limited recollection of this repertoire, and those younger than 40 years essentially "didn't know nothing." Why? What happened to this genre of literature that so perfectly fostered musical growth in infants and toddlers?

During the past 100 years families have been redefined. Members of the extended families, often including several generations, once lived near each other and interacted. Today, the extended family is geographically dispersed and the nuclear family—parents(s) and children—is separate and smaller. This shift in family community has strained the old traditions. Playful songs and rhymes of community affection and endorsement, once orally transmitted to each new generation, are nearly forgotten. Commercially imposed "ear candy" gives a temporary rush but lacks the lasting nutritional value of the literature whose place it usurps.

If children are to develop healthy bodies, they must be nurtured with healthy food and exercise. Similarly, quality language usage and literature affects children's speech, vocabulary, reading habits and musical growth.

- If children are to develop correct grammar, clear enunciation, and a sophisticated vocabulary, they must hear these language patterns in their daily lives. If they hear incorrect grammar, poor enunciation, and a limited vocabulary, they will assimilate these language patterns.
- If children experience expressive speaking and are read to in an expressive voice, they will later read aloud and to themselves with appropriate expression.

- If children are to grow into adults who cherish reading and good books, they must be nurtured with excellent children's music that is sung with sensitivity and musical expression.

So, what is good literature? There are several criteria that can be useful when selecting music for the young child. Of primary importance in the use of songs and rhymes is a text that relates to early childhood's joy in *make-believe*: words that invite the child into fanciful adventures: riding a horse, playing with a pet, encountering imaginary creatures through songs and rhymes. Good children's books are "wonder-full": filled with wonder. They are interesting to adults as well as to children and they remain so after numerous readings.

Good children's songs demonstrate similar qualities. They are wonder-full, they appeal to adults and children, and they are still pleasurable to sing after many repetitions. If a song loses its appeal quickly—like chewing gum that loses its flavor—it is probably neither good nor worthwhile.

The words of the song should be childlike, but not childish. The rhythm should be close to the rhythm that would naturally occur if speaking the words. The melody should serve as an extension of the natural expressiveness of the spoken line. The relationship between the words and the melody should embody all the subtleties of natural spoken inflections, with ups and downs, dramatic moments and intensification repose patterns like those in expressive speech.

Melody emerges naturally from language in folksongs. To test the relationship between words and melody, read the words aloud, like a poem. Where do the spoken rhythm and pitch inflections occur? Does the melody enhance those natural inflections or does it undermine the expressive potential? For example, the words and melody of "Frère Jacques" ask a question in the second phrase: "Dormez-vous *(mi-fa-sol)?*" The melody rises, like the natural inflection of the voice. When sung with English words, however, the text begins with a *question,* "Are you sleeping?" but is sung to a melodic *statement (do-re-mi-do).* This mix-match of words and melody undermines an opportunity to influence the growth of expressive sensitivity.

The singer must bring the song to life. The text may be wonder-full and the melody natural to the pitch and rhythmic inflections of speech, but the printed score is little more than a musical skeleton. Notation is not music. To sing songs as printed on the page is like reading stories aloud with no inflection. A good reader brings printed words to life through expressive speech; an artistic singer has an intuition for nuances that bring a song to life. Children learn to read aloud expressively by hearing stories that are read expressively. Children learn to sing expressively by hearing models of expressive singing. Children must be sung to with appropriate expression in order to nurture their instinct for musical expressiveness.

Our grandparents' songs and rhymes have continuing value: they are filled with wonder, they blend words and music expressively, and they are still delicious after many singings. We should nurture children with music that has emerged naturally out of human expression rather than accepting contrived songs that have emerged from commercial interests. Zoltán Kodály, who completed his studies first in linguistics and later in musicology; urged repeatedly that quality literature was essential in Hungarian schools.

> So by communicating only inferior music…the schools cut off the way to a higher development of the musical sense. In the name of good taste and of the Hungarian spirit alike, school literature generally used today must be protested against. I include in this the greater part of unison songs, too. Some writers of textbooks consider Hungarian children idiotic by tutoring them with such little verses and songs as could be improvised much better by any sound child given the chance.[2]

In another presentation he added the following:

> It is not advisable to peruse [these] collections. At first one laughs, then one becomes annoyed, and finally one despairs and cannot imagine that in a country where such things are printed and even sung aloud, there may still be room for anything better. And what about the masses for whom this remains their only music? Can we be surprised if, by the time they grow up, they cannot get any further than the music of the trashiest hit?[3]

But What Can We Teach a One-Year-Old to Do?

The infant's job is to make sense out of the world. While their neurological networks are maturing, infants encounter many sounds to decode—including language and music. The child learns to make sense out of words, even before developing the ability to speak any of those words. Effort causes linguistic synapses to be stimulated which

in turn, signals the brain to maintain these pathways for future use.

By 6 months of age, infants in English-speaking homes already have different auditory maps—as shown by electrical measurements that identify which neurons respond to different sounds—from those in Swedish-speaking homes. Children are functionally deaf to sounds absent from their native tongue. The map is completed by the first birthday. "By 12 months," says Patricia Kuhl of the University of Washington, "infants have lost their ability to discriminate sounds that are not significant in their language, and their babbling has acquired the sound of their language."[4]

Similarly, infants need to hear and feel music early on if they are to begin to make sense of it. Neurological pathways, when not built early, become increasingly difficult to build later. The time to start building and maintaining those information highways is during the first months of life.

In an earlier article, I compared nurturing the child's developing mind to growing vegetables in a garden.[5] Initially we may plant more seeds than we expect to harvest. When the plants begin to grow, we thin out those that show the least promise so that the more promising plants have sufficient space and nutrients to prosper. Seeds neglected during the early stages of germination seldom recover fully. Though the plants should never be neglected, neglect during the beginning stages of development is more detrimental than neglect during the later weeks of summer.

The child's brain begins with an abundance of neural pathways. Pathways that show the most promise are maintained and intensified. Those that are neglected atrophy. It is during the first two years of life that the brain will begin to determine which seeds to nurture—according to the available experiences. In his landmark book, *Frames of Mind,* Howard Gardner reports the following:

> …in human beings the density of synapses increases sharply during the first months of life, reaches a maximum at the ages of 1 to 2 (roughly 50% above the adult mean density), declines between the ages of 2 and 16, and remains relatively constant until the age of 72.[6]

Jane Healy makes a similar comment in her book, *Endangered Minds:*

> The strength and efficiency of synaptic connections determine the speed and power with which your brain functions. The most important news about

synapses is that they are formed, strengthened, and maintained by interaction with experience.[7]

Organization inhibits reorganization. It is more difficult to reorganize a brain than to organize it in the first place. Carving out neuronal tracks for certain types of learning is best accomplished when the synaptic connections for that particular skill are being formed, before they "firm-up" around certain types of responses.

In the same book, Jane Healy presents the concept of "two directional" thinking and provides a considerable amount of support for the need to evoke responses from children. Information that only travels "in" (as in most television viewing) does not promote the necessary brain activity to nurture synaptic development. Learning that evokes responses from the child promotes the appropriate brain activity to stimulate synaptic growth. Healy quotes Phyllis Weikart:

> Feeling (the beat) has to be independent for the child: you can't make it loud and you can't make it visual as in videos: it has to be felt. Unless the child is rocked, patted, stroked, danced with at the same time, unless adults are creating the feel of the beat for the child who is hearing it, that feel of beat does not develop.[8]

Applied to music learning, these fascinating concepts explain the importance of appropriate musical experiences during the first two years. During these years, when the mind is making sense of the world, musical syntax is developing. Beat, meter, rhythm, tonality, and expressive sensitivity should be presented. Would you not talk to a baby simply because he or she cannot talk? Then why wait until the child can sing and move to introduce music?

One hundred years ago families nurtured infants and toddlers with rhymes, songs and activities that developed children's innate musicality. Today's parents of infants and toddlers need to be reintroduced to these wonder-full songs and rhymes. Classes shared by parents, infants and toddlers provide needed opportunities to rediscover excellent songs and rhymes that develop the musical mind.

What Might an Infant/Toddler Music and Movement Class Look Like?

In classes of infants and toddlers with their parents, the toddlers and infants respond differently to the same repertoire of songs, rhymes and activities. Infants from birth to age 18 months are often passive observers. Toddlers of 18–24 months take a more active role. Planned repetition of appropriate experiences during the first 18 months prepares the infant to respond naturally later on—during the toddler months. To gain awareness of beat, young children should experience the feeling of beat while the mind is still organizing. To prepare an accurate singing voice, infants and toddlers should hear much accurate singing. To find expressivity in singing and moving to music, children must have music and movement presented to them in an expressive manner during their early years.

Older adults of today recall many songs, rhymes and games that adults taught and played with infants and toddlers in a bygone era. Today, classes that present appropriate repertoire for adults to share with infants and toddlers can generate similar growth in musicality. Today's young children can easily assimilate beat, meter, melody, tonality, wonder, and expressive sensitivity through songs, rhymes, and games like those that generations of children have experienced in the past.

Bounces
Bouncing an infant or toddler on the knee is the adult–child activity most often recalled by the elderly. Bounces provide an ideal experience of the beat for young children. These wonder-full rhymes and songs, which embody make-believe as they provide an opportunity to learn beat and meter, often consist of delightful melodies.

> To market, to market
> To buy a fat pig.
> Home again, home again
> Jiggity-jig.

Newborn babies enjoy bounces, and so do toddlers. The adult may sit on the floor or in a chair. Seated on the floor, with legs stretched out and the infant on his or her lap, the adult recites the rhyme, lifting the knees on the beat. When seated in a chair, the adult lifts his or her heels in rhythm with the beat. A baby that can support his/her head may sit on an adult's knee. (If the toddler's feet can touch the floor during the bounce, the floor position is better because it will encourage the child's motion of pushing off from the floor to the beat.) Be sure to adjust the tempo of the song or rhyme so as to complement the tempo of the child's movement.

Wiggles
Chant a rhyme as you wiggle each of the child's fingers or toes from largest to smallest. The rhyme

"This Little Piggy Went to Market" is one that most elders who were interviewed could recall, but there are dozens of others, and all have elements of wonder for the young child.

> This little pig danced a merry, merry jig,
> This little pig ate candy.
> This little pig wore a blue and yellow wig,
> This little pig was a dandy.
> But this little pig never grew to be big,
> So they called him tiny little Andy.

Wiggle a younger infant's toes rather than the fingers, keeping in mind that a clenched fist is characteristic of the newborn. As maturation takes place, infants will allow their fingers to be wiggled in rhythm with the beat. Toddlers can wiggle your fingers as you chant the rhyme. Take care to follow each child's demonstrated tempo.

Tickles

Trace a circle in the palm of a young child, then walk your fingers up the baby's arm in rhythm with the beat. End with a gentle tickle.

> Round and round the cornfield
> Looking for a hare.
> Where can we find one?
> Right up there.

If the infant is reluctant to open his or her hand, you can place the child in your lap and gently tap a circular pattern on the infant's stomach. Let older infants and toddlers take an active role: ask them to trace a circle in your hand and "walk" the beat up your arm.

Tapping

Adults and babies often share in a tapping game. The adult taps the baby's foot in rhythm with the beat of the song or rhyme. The activity may include gently tapping on the face or another part of the body as well as tapping the child's foot.

> Shoe a little horse,
> Shoe a little mare.
> But let the little colt
> Go bare, bare, bare.

Initially the adult taps on the infant's foot; encourage toddlers to tap on themselves or on the bottom of the adult's foot.

Clapping

There are only a few songs or rhymes for clapping with baby. "Pat-a Cake" is a favorite, as it was many years ago:

> Pat-a-cake, pat-a-cake, baker's man
> Bake me a cake as fast as you can.
> Roll it and pat it and mark it with a "B,"
> And put it in the oven for baby and me.

Although these games are sometimes performed with the adult holding onto the child's hands, with children older than 6 months it is better to evoke a movement response from the child: Place the child's hands in a palms-down position, then tap on the child's palm. Soon the child will begin tapping down on the palm of the adult. Be sure to sing or chant the rhyme in tempo with the baby's movements. Remember, holding and moving the child's hands to "help" him/her feel the beat is like holding the baby's lips and moving them up and down to say "mama."

Simple Songs

Even though very young children cannot sing complex songs, they should hear many songs, both simple and complex. Most songs used in teaching bounces, wiggles, tickles, tapping, and clapping have melodies that are too difficult for the 2½-year-old to sing. One solution is to use simple, singable songs such as "Rain Rain Go Away" for a portion of each lesson.

> Rain, rain
> Go away—
> Come again
> Some other day

The adult should not be disappointed if the infant or toddler does not join in singing during this time. Plant the songs in the child's memory for harvest later on, when the child discovers his or her singing voice.

Simple Circles

Introduce simple circle games to children who can toddle about, with or without assistance from an adult. Circle games add structure to songs that end with a surprise lift or "fall down."

> Three times around went our gallant ship,
> And three times around went she.
> Three times around went our gallant ship,
> And she sank to the bottom of the sea.

Each toddler walks around a circle with an adult. (Walk side-by-side with the toddler or just behind to provide additional balance.) Toddlers find it difficult to twist their bodies while holding hands with others in a circle; therefore it is best if they form the circle without holding hands. Simply walk in the direction the toes are pointing, without holding hands.

Movement With Recorded Music

Include a recording of worthwhile folk, classical, or jazz music in each lesson so that the adults can dance with their infants or toddlers. Choose recorded selections not longer than 2–3 minutes and with a tempo in the range of 120 to 136 taps per minute (about two taps per second). The infants, held next to an adult's shoulder, feel the beat as it is tapped lightly on their back, while the adult paces around the room. Toddlers able to stand by themselves can observe and learn to imitate the simple motions performed by the adults. The toddlers may bounce from their knees, tap on their legs, swing their arms, twist from their waist, shake hands, tap on the floor, or rock from side to side.

Lullabies

Lullabies are among the most musical of all song experiences for young children. Even several years of lessons would give too little time to share all of the beautiful lullaby melodies. Lullabies increase melodic awareness and perception, develop a sense of beat and tempo, and most of all, convey musical expressiveness.

> Hush a-bye, don't you cry
> Go to sleep, little baby.
> When you wake, you shall have,
> All the pretty little horses.
> Blacks and bays, dapples and grays,
> All the pretty little horses.
> Hush a-bye, don't you cry,
> go to sleep, little baby.

Try ending each lesson with a lullaby. After singing the lullaby several times, repeat it, this time, humming the tune. The magic spell cast by wordless humming can be a peak experience in the musical nurturing of young children.

Promoting musical development is necessary if infants' and toddlers' neural pathways are to develop for later musical sensitivity. Many believe that attention to the musical nurturing of infants and toddlers may even affect the future for audiences in concert halls. Nurturing certainly will affect the musical life of the child. The songs and rhymes shared by parents and children many years ago are still appropriate for today's infants and toddlers, who can benefit greatly from the heritage of natural play and wonder-full rhymes and music that were once a regular part of childhood. Our forebears intuitively shared these songs and rhymes with their children. Somehow, they just seemed to know what was right.

Notes

1. For the past 15 years I have made a concerted effort to interview senior citizens concerning what they remembered about playing with infants. I would ask them the same question: "Do you remember any songs or games that you played with baby in your lap?" My graduate students have also interviewed seniors using this question. The results were the same: those over the age of 80 had the largest repertoire of songs and games to play with baby.

2. Zoltán Kodály, "Children's Choirs," in *The Selected Writings of Zoltán Kodály* (London: Boosey and Hawkes 1974), 125.

3. Zoltán Kodály, "Music in the Kindergarten," in *The Selected Writings of Zoltán Kodály* (London: Boosey and Hawkes 1974), 142.

4. Sharon Begley, "Your Child's Brain," *Newsweek,* 19 February 1996, 57.

5. John M. Feierabend, "Music and Intelligence in the Early Years," *Early Childhood Connections* 1, no. 2 (1995): 5–13.

6. Howard Gardner, *Frames of Mind* (New York: Basic Books, 1983), 44–45.

7. Jane Healy, *Endangered Minds* (New York: Touchstone Books, 1990), 53–54.

8. Ibid., 172.

John M. Feierabend is director of the Music Education Division at the Hartt School of the University of Hartford in Connecticut and director of the National Center for Music and Movement in the Early Years. This article, which appeared in the October 1997 issue of the North Dakota Music Educator, *was originally published in the Fall 1996 issue of* Early Childhood Connections. *Reprinted by permission of* Early Childhood Connections: Journal of Music- and Movement-Based Learning. *ISSN 1085-522x ©2000 by Foundation of Music Based Learning, PO Box 4274, Greensboro, NC 27404 (Phone: 336-272-5303).*

Early Childhood Music Field Experience: Instrument Petting Zoo

by Linda Hartley and Instrumental Music Pedagogy Class Members

OCMEA (Ohio Collegiate Music Educators Association) members at the University of Dayton (UD) initiated and participated in an "Instrument Petting Zoo," at their campus Children's Center. As a part of an instrumental methods class assignment, junior music education majors brought a variety of instruments to the classrooms of 2- to 5-year-old children. The purpose of this assignment was two-fold: 1) to introduce instruments to young children; and 2) to allow music education majors to work with pre-school age children. Most of the music education students had not worked with this age group.

Instruments used included an electronic keyboard, violin, cello, trombone, trumpet, saxophone, clarinet, flute, and cymbals. Each child had the opportunity to explore these instruments in a variety of ways. Children could touch the instruments, discovering moving parts, and could play the instrument as well. UD students spent approximately 15 minutes in each of four classrooms, rotating rooms for an hour so that all classes could experience each instrument.

The following are a few of the comments made by the UD students following this field experience:

"Working with these young children was one of those times when I was positive that I am in the right field. The children's reactions to being able to play the instruments were really exciting. It was interesting to see the big gap between the 2- to 3-year-olds and the 3- to 4-year-olds. The younger ones were often more timid and it was harder to keep their attention. The older ones were right there. They wanted to see and touch everything and try everything over and over. The excitement level was very high. Many of them have seen the UD Marching Band practice in the field across their playground fence and they expressed that it was neat to get to play the instruments they have seen but never played before." (Andrea Krile)

"Young children are like sponges. They love new experiences and absorb so much information. Since many of the children we worked with had never seen real instruments before, there was a definite sense of amazement and awe. Pre-school age children are willing and excited to explore new things, especially music." (Sarah Ford)

"The interest level of the children was amazing. Most of them couldn't wait to get their hands on the violin. Some were so eager to play the instrument that they had difficulty following my directions. However, once the children had the experience of playing the violin, several of them came back for more. I never thought pre-school age children would remain focused and interested in something for up to fifteen minutes. One highlight for me was the reaction of one little girl's mom. She was pleased that we came to provide this musical instrument experience for her child. After the mother dropped off her child at the Children's Center, she stayed in the classroom the entire time we were there. I was pleased to see a parent value the importance of music experiences for her child." (Aja Glett)

"We accidentally went into the 1- to 2-year-old class, but I'm glad that we did. At first the children were scared of the instruments (violin and cello); they didn't want to touch them. Gradually they approached and would pluck a string or touch the bow and then run away. One child, who wouldn't leave the teacher's lap, eventually was running the bow across the strings by the time we were ready to leave." (Stephanie Gist)

All UD students who participated agreed that this was a valuable experience for them. While this project was designed for the young child, it would be successful for any age, including senior adults. We recommend and encourage other OCMEA chapters to incorporate an "Instrument Petting Zoo" at your school!

Linda Hartley is associate professor of music education at the University of Dayton in Ohio. This article originally appeared in the April 2000 issue of Ohio's Triad. *Reprinted by permission.*

Let's Playfully Sing: Teaching Singing to Preschoolers

by Owen Wingate

Take a visit to a preschool, daycare, or Headstart facility and you will most likely hear young children singing. For most children, the pairing of words with a tune seems to come naturally. They sing songs that they have learned at home and in community groups or religious organizations. You may hear them sing at almost any time during the day. Most children will sing many times each day.

- They sing alone while swinging back and forth on the swing set.
- They sing and chant in groups playing on the playground.
- They sing while playing with manipulatives, dolls, puppets and other toys.
- They sing and hum as they listen to "quiet time" or "rest time" music.

However, during your visit you may notice that some children are not singing, that some are "shout-singing," or that most of the singing could be improved. Some children have no parent whose singing they can model. They do not see or hear their parents or caregivers singing, and therefore they are reluctant to sing themselves. Most preschoolers who do try to sing produce vocal sounds in either a breathy voice or a talking/shouting voice. As music educators we should help young children to find their singing voices and teach them to sing in a healthy and expressive manner.

This can be accomplished in a playful, child-centered manner that does not impose adult-styled voice lessons, which are inappropriate for the preschool singer. This article highlights some useful methods, techniques, and resources that are appropriate for early childhood music teachers interested in teaching children to sing better.

When and How?

Because it is generally agreed that singing is at the core of music education for all children, careful attention should be given to teaching this important psychomotor skill in the child's early years. Many educators and voice teachers believe that one should wait until after puberty for formal training and that young children should just sing songs! This is called the song method, and it has prevailed in schools for most of the 20th century.

Some music teachers believe that voice training, which includes respect for the child's vocal mechanism along with developmentally appropriate techniques, can and should be taught during early childhood in the preschool or daycare.

Learning in the early years can involve singing and play. In the preschool and kindergarten years, learning, singing, and play are almost synonymous. Teachers use singing as a "fun way" to learn the alphabet, numbers, colors, shapes, etc. Piggyback songbooks use well-known tunes as a delivery vehicle for all sorts of information that young children need to learn. Some parents croon lullabies and sing songs to relax, soothe, reassure, and entertain their children.

Many songs from television shows, radio jingles, and religious settings often contain inappropriate vocal models/ranges and sound tracks that may confuse the young singer or inhibit the exploration and discovery of the child singing voice. The question remains: do teachers, music educators or parents teach young children to sing and sing correctly? Unfortunately, most teachers, music educators and parents assume that their children learn to sing automatically and correctly by singing songs.

The Child Voice

We have all heard children, and even adolescents, who sing using their speaking voice or only their chest voice. This may result in the child entering elementary school with poor singing skills and unhealthy singing habits.

Most younger children who discover their singing voice use only a portion of their possible range and color. When they move on to elementary school, they may become discouraged and stop singing altogether when:

- they cannot perform higher pitches with their lower or middle register
- they can't sing loudly with their high, head voice
- they cannot accurately match pitch.

These children are sometimes labeled as inaccurate singers, nonsingers, or "monotones," and teachers assign them to play rhythm instruments or some other non-singing part in the class musical production.

One of the goals of early childhood music education is to teach children to find and use the singing voice. How does the teacher encourage young children to explore and exercise the voice?

What are some techniques that music teachers can use to assist and help young children find and use their whole singing voice? And finally, what materials or methods exist to facilitate this type of teaching?

When singing with young children music teachers must think of singing as "playing with the voice." The first phrase that comes to mind is "make it fun." Turning learning into a game and blending learning with play is instinctual for many early childhood teachers.

Singing at any age requires singers to maintain good body posture; support breathing using the diaphragm and intercostels; hear the pitch and rhythm in their minds; phonate sound using the vocal folds; sustain a resonate sound; and articulate vowels and consonants with expression. Young children can develop healthy vocal habits and singing technique through simple vocal exercises that encourage growth in each of the above areas. These exercises should not be rigorous, adult-style vocalizing. Rather, they are light, head-voice oriented and can be incorporated into story time, reading, movement, games and drama.

One approach which integrates singing skills with language arts is *The Sound Concept: Preparing the Young Voice for Singing* by Judy Carol Thompson. The kit includes a direction booklet, a series of flash cards, and evaluation forms. "Big book" story books may also be ordered which use the same characters introduced on the flash cards. Children respond to the pictures on the flash cards and in the "big-book" stories with teacher directed or modeled vocal sounds by playful vocal exploration in seven categories:

1. Descending and ascending sounds
2. Breathing and breath support
3. Round, pure vowel sounds
4. Glissandi
5. Short, heady sounds
6. Resonance
7. Minor third intervals.

Drama and character role play is also a part of these vocal exercises and warm-ups. Children are asked to imitate not only vocal sounds but also facial actions and body movements. Thompson believes that tension in the voice can be lessened when the cushion of air carries the tone and the face is activated with "lifted eyebrows, a glisten in the eyes, and a lift to the cheeks." A detailed progress report can be given to parents on forms with the flash cards and story books.

Another resource is the book *One, Two Three… Echo Me!* by Loretta Mitchell. The author includes a section of activities to help children differentiate between the speaking and singing voices and exercises for younger and older children. There are also games and activities for pitch matching, as well as extensive teaching suggestions and ideas.

Many children's games and toys may be used to teach basic voice production in singing.

- Marionettes can be used to demonstrate good posture and correct singing position. Standing and "reaching for the stars" or stretching upwards like a tree are beginning points.
- Toy pinwheels which may be purchased in any toy store can be used to demonstrate focused breath expiration. Young children need to see the power of their invisible breath. The air they breathe in and the air they breathe out is abstract and not a part of their reality until they can see it move a pinwheel or fill a balloon or blow a bubble. After seeing these demonstrations, it is important for them to verbalize and discuss the experiments. Then the children will begin to "own" this knowledge and make use of it in singing.
- A balloon may be used by the music teacher to demonstrate a full breath and the principle of air-driven vibration of the vocal folds. Blow up the balloon and discuss the full expansion and roundness of the balloon shape. Demonstrate a full diaphragmatic breath placing your hand on your midriff abdominal area to show expansion and fullness. Compare this to the balloon. Easy-to-blow balloons can be effective. However, younger children should not be given balloons to inflate. They may accidentally swallow or choke on them.
- Blowing out the candles on a birthday cake demonstrates a forceful airstream. Blowing a candle flame until it only flickers or gently blowing a feather demonstrates increased breath control.

Some toys and materials inherently encourage and enhance vocal play.

- Toy microphones which reverberate without electrical amplification can be used to enhance the softer voice and encourage role playing.
- Actual microphones that work with a tape recorder can be used.
- Some battery driven microphones work with a radio on an FM band.

- Tape recording each voice and the class singing can promote interest.
- Video recording a child singing or a class performing generates attention.
- PVC "U" shape pipe connectors and toy telephones allow for self-monitoring and may encourage children to experiment with the voice.
- The expandable, plastic venting used to connect clothes dryers to outside vents allows children to "play telephone" or sing and talk with each other across the room.

Character Play

Imitating character voices while storytelling, reading books, and role-playing or drama can also be used to teach about singing and the voice. Children love to hear stories read or told expressively, with vocal inflection. They also enjoy trying to imitate character voices. One way to encourage vocal inflection is through floor play with plastic action figures, dolls and puppets based on characters from books, cartoons or movies. Current favorites are Disney movie and Saturday morning cartoon characters. Many of these plastic figures have mouths which open and close. This enables the child to manipulate them in a puppet-like way while speaking or singing.

It has been said that music and singing lessons for the child should begin nine months before birth! That means that mom and dad should be singers, the home should be filled with music, and that they should reserve a place in a preschool, daycare, or Headstart class that will teach and encourage singing as a part of their unborn child's early education. As music educators, our responsibility is to teach singing and provide an appropriate music education for all preschool children.

Owen Wingate is professor of music at Lake City Community College in Lake City, Florida. This article originally appeared in the January 1997 issue of the Florida Music Director. *Reprinted by permission.*

Kid-Tested Ideas that Work for the Young and Special Learner
by Leona Frances Woskowiak

It is very important to begin musical training at an early age because children are capable of absorbing things at a much faster rate when they are young. This early training is also important for the special learner. Whether a teacher is working with young or special children, the key to success involves the use of small steps and repetition. Children learn at different rates and in many different ways and so it is crucial to the learning process to constantly remind ourselves that experience and involvement are key words in this process.

As children experience learning, they remember ten percent of what they read, twenty percent of what they hear, and thirty percent of what they see. In addition, they remember fifty percent of what they hear and see, seventy percent of what they say, and ninety percent of what they say and do.

Movement Activities

Skills that are developed through movement activities are basic to the musical training of all children. All activities are completed using small steps and repetition. Movement activities should begin with movements within a small area such as their own world, balloon, etc., before they are expanded to larger areas. To assist the children, puppets and stuffed animals may be used to encourage a variety of movements. In addition to these activities, children enjoy a trip to the Magic Jungle where they become the animals within the jungle. Four animals are used to introduce the four basic note values in common meter. The activity names of walk, run-run, step-bounce and step bounce-bounce-bounce are the favorite movement steps of the tiger (walk), mouse (run-run), baby elephant (step-bounce), and the old, fat elephant (step bounce-bounce-bounce).

Children move as they chant the activity names of each of the animals and later this movement becomes a prereading activity. The tiger movement of "walk" is shown on a chart as four consecutive tiger paw prints and the children chant this as "walk-walk-walk-walk." This type of chanting is considered a beginning reading activity using four quarter notes. Later the activity names of the other three animals are added to their "music reading" vocabulary. The mouse chart shows eight small mouse paw prints; the baby elephant shows two medium elephant foot prints; and the old elephant chart shows one large elephant foot print. Both young and special children respond to this type of activity because they are involved in the story of the animals and are not aware that they are actually reading rhythms.

Expanding a Story

The children enjoy the expansion of this story to the Magic Moon Jungle. As the tiger moves through his Magic Jungle he sees another jungle hovering overhead and realizes that it is a space ship from the moon. He sees a moon tiger peering over the edge of the moon jungle and decides to say "hello." Unfortunately, the moon tiger does not understand him. The tiger thinks and thinks and decides to communicate with the moon tiger by taking four steps as he chants "walk-walk-walk-walk." The moon tiger gets excited when he sees and hears this and decides that he will also take four steps as he chats "ta-ta-ta-ta." As he does this, a picture of four quarter note stems come out of his mouth.

The earth tiger is totally surprised by this and decides that he must visit Mr. Marshall Music and ask him about this phenomenon. Mr. Music informs him that he has seen and heard "moon talk." In moon talk, "walk" is a "ta" and the stems that he saw is called magic moon code. Every time an animal in the Magic Moon Jungle moves and chants his special activity, the magic code comes out of his mouth.

The mouse comes to the Magic Jungle to join the tiger and as he looks up, he sees the moon mouse. The mouse decides to follow the plan that was used by the tiger. He steps and chants eight "run-run's" and then the moon mouse steps and chants eight "ti-ti's" as the eighth note stems come out of his mouth. The next step involves the reading of the moon code. Young and special children have experienced and enjoyed much success with this type of reading.

Problem Solving

Movement in a circle can be made more interesting by giving the children problems to solve as they are moving. Problems that they enjoy solving might be marching with one wooden leg, a leg that is made of cooked spaghetti, or knees made of wiggling jello. Exploring this type of movement activity assists the student in developing thinking skills. The children often suggest new ways to move. They also enjoy having their movement guided by the use of large arrows that the teacher uses to indicate directional movement in the circle. A prerecorded tape is played as the arrow instructs them to move left, right, up, or down.

Language Development

Language development is directly associated with activities that are included in rhythmic reading. One such activity is the fruit chant. While seated in a circle, the children are shown two pieces of fruit, a pear and an apple. They are asked to identify the pear and how many sounds are in the word "pear." They are instructed to chant the name of the fruit each time that it is shown to them. The teacher guides them in chanting "pear" in a steady quarter-note beat pattern. Later they are shown the apple; they identify it and indicate that it has two sounds. They chant "apple" as the teacher guides them in chanting the two sounds in a steady beat pattern. The chanting is reinforced by patting the one and two syllable words on the floor.

After successfully completing this activity, the children are shown fruit charts. Each chart has four pieces of the same kind of fruit and before they chant the name of the fruit, they determine that they will chant the name of the fruit four times. The early charts have one syllable fruits such as pear, grapes, peach, and plum. After they "read" each separate chart, they read them in order, establishing a two-, three-, etc., measure chant.

Follow up charts include two-syllable fruits such as apple, lemon, etc. These are "read" as separate four-beat charts and then they are read as two-, three-, etc., measure chants. Once the children have spent time learning the separate one- and two- syllable fruits, the fruits are combined. For example, an early chart shows pear, pear, apple, pear. The teacher guides the children in discovering that one- and two- syllable fruits may be combined in a chant. As the children continue to chant these charts, they are establishing a solid foundation and understanding of two basic note values in common meter.

Children may also be introduced to rests in music with the fruit charts. The children are shown a chart with four apples and they "read" the chart using the word "apple." Later, they are shown a second chart with three apples and an apple core. They determine that when they are finished eating an apple they have a core that must be thrown away. The children clap and chant "apple" three times and then they "throw away" the core by throwing their arms out to either side indicating a rest. These activities prepare the students for future music reading activities. They have been used successfully with both young and special children.

One final suggestion for keeping the children on task and focused is through the use of a large square that is red on one side and green on the other. They are shown the red side of the square when it is the teacher's turn to talk, sing, give instructions, etc. The green side is shown when it is the children's turn to complete the task at hand.

Through the use of these suggestions, teachers will find a higher level of motivation on the part of the children and a refreshing "breath of spring" in their own daily lessons.

Leona Woskowiak is professor emeritus of music education at Millersville University and a minister of music in Lancaster, Pennsylvania. This article originally appeared in the May 1997 issue of Pennsylvania's PMEA News. *Reprinted by permission.*

Section 3

Assessment

Assessment of the music learning that takes place in an early childhood setting is essential to the success of any program. In this section, the reader will find helpful suggestions of ways to approach this task.

 Section 3

Assessment

Is Assessment in Music Appropriate in the Early Childhood Years?
by Frances Rauscher

Assessment in music is often overlooked or avoided in the early childhood years because it appears to be incompatible with a child-centered, process-oriented philosophy which is characteristic of education for young children. A reflective assessment procedure, however, can inform the early childhood teacher's practice of guiding learning in music. Artistic profiles of individual children's accomplishments can center on processes such as discovery, pursuit, perception, communication, self- and social-awareness, skill use, creativity, analysis, and critique. Qualitative, observation-based assessment provides a means with which to provide feedback to children, parents, and educational administrators about individual and group achievements.

In a comprehensive early childhood educational program, children learn to make sense of their worlds through controlled attempts to explore, develop, and express ideas and concepts through performance and action (Alper, 1987; Smith, 1980). In all subject areas, the emphasis is on learning through direct experience and experimentation. The same is true in music, where the learning process revolves around acting-out: using the body and voice to imagine and to represent meaning through the integration of thoughts, sensations, and symbol systems. Often learning is a private experience, but teachers can assist young children to develop complex musical skills, such as discrimination, through the development of a musical vocabulary and through reflection upon the creative process, aesthetic qualities, evaluation of products, and recognition that there is no one right way to answer a musical problem.

The products or actions of a child, however, can only provide an impression of what the child has learned during a musical experience.

Therefore, to review a child's knowledge of music based on the product alone would overlook other important components of musicality and the complex, multi-levelled skills that are involved in learning. For young children in particular, music must be conceived as a total and integrated experience which warrants the employment of a global form of assessment (McLeod, 1990). Evidence for evaluation and reflection must be gathered over a period of time and focus on numerous musical experiences and works. The manner in which this is achieved is a complex process, one which is made difficult in the early childhood years by the need for the teacher to make sensitive interpretations of children's behavior.

Observation and Interpretation as a Basis for Assessment and Evaluation
In early childhood education, assessment is closely linked to program evaluation. On a daily basis, the teacher plans the curriculum and makes evaluations and programming changes that are based upon young children's learning. In other words, what the child gains from one experience helps the teacher to determine the next learning event. When working with older children, the process of evaluation and program development is made easy by the students' ability to reflect on and discuss their work, often undertaken as long-term projects. The limited verbal skills of young children and the relatively short duration of activities, however, require the teacher to interpret behavior and learning outcomes on the basis of observations which are considered within the context of the cognitive, social, and physical development of young children.

The majority of evaluation and assessment procedures used in early childhood education derive from phenomenological and qualitative-naturalistic traditions (Alexander, 1982; Almy & Genishi, 1979). Participant observation in classrooms requires the same data collection techniques that are used in other settings, including interviewing, observing, documenting, and analyzing products, and counting events. These techniques enable the teacher-investigator to understand the meaning of musical experiences through the eyes of the child-participant. This requires the adult to adopt the child's perspective: to think, imagine, perceive, fantasize, create, conceptualize, and use symbols as the child would.

General Artistic Processes That Are Applicable to Music

Nine general artistic processes can be identified which closely resemble the musical interests and abilities of young children. These processes have been implied or described in part by several writers (see e.g., Gardner, 1990; McArdle & Barker, 1990), and are outlined below:

1. *Discovery:* involves observing, exploring options with a range of materials, comparing, questioning, seeing possibilities, finding alternatives, and seeking purpose.
2. *Pursuit:* involves entering into musical activities, taking initiative, focusing on specific ideas, exploring in depth, staying on task, being goal directed, problem solving, generating ideas and carrying them out, working hard, and developing a musical idea over time or around personal themes.
3. *Perception:* involves showing sensory awareness, illustrating sensitivity to physical properties and qualities of materials and the environment, "hearing inside the head," internalizing movement, making fine discriminations, showing care and attention to detail, and evidencing sensitivity to a variety of genres, cultures, and historical periods.
4. *Communication:* involves selecting and using musical materials and elements with intent, expressing ideas or feeling through the musical medium, and using symbols.
5. *Self- and Social-Awareness:* involves working independently, tapping into personal feelings, participating in preparation and clean-up, sharing discoveries, tolerating frustration, participating in group activities, cooperating, communicating effectively, negotiating, empathizing, appreciating other people's contributions, and making suggestions.
6. *Skill Use:* involves manipulating materials; showing muscular coordination; controlling basic techniques; showing sensitivity to the elements, principles, and processes of music; show-

ing aesthetic sensitivity; and demonstrating a sense of standards and quality.
7. *Creativity:* involves responding to different situations flexibly, seeing afresh, enjoying, taking risks with the musical medium, using imagination, and showing inventiveness.
8. *Transfer:* involves describing to others what is seen, heard, felt, thought, or imagined; articulating musical goals; reflecting on process and product; showing interest in hearing and using musical terminology; relating learning to previous learning; contributing own opinions; and changing direction and attitudes if necessary.
9. *Critique:* involves appreciating artistic products; talking about one's own artistry and the works of peers; accepting and incorporating suggestions where appropriate; using the processes of describing, interpreting, and judging; and using the work of others for ideas and inspiration.

While a hierarchy within the list is not implied—each aspect being important in itself—there is an implicit order of complexity. Critiquing, for example, requires a higher-level skill than Discovery. Yet, even young children demonstrate the ability to critique (Cole & Schaefer, 1990). The process or processes used in any activity will also depend on the child's developmental level. In addition, each descriptor has meaning only when viewed in the context of the learning environment, teaching practices and methods, and curriculum organization and content. For example, Discovery will be more easily achieved in a learning environment in which children are encouraged to ask questions, explore ideas, and imagine new possibilities than in one in which such processes are not valued.

These nine processes can be used as a basis for assessment, although they are not a prescriptive framework for assessment. They can help teachers to understand musical processes, to recognize how they are used by young children, to focus on processes which will assist children to learn about music, and to explain children's musical development to parents and others.

In addition, the list can be used as a basis for interacting with, or providing feedback to children about their musical experiences and products. The most valuable feedback that a child can receive are comments that occur during, or immediately after, a child's musical experience and involve reflection upon what the child has produced and experienced rather than those which are information-giving. For example, rather than asking a child to name the notes being played, the teacher might ask open-ended questions and model, label, and extend the child's present understanding. In other words, whether a child is creating a rhythmic pattern on a drum or singing to a CD, comments such as "Good girl!" or "Excellent work!" may be encouraging, but they are not descriptive or explanatory, nor do they enhance a child's awareness of musical processes, elements, concepts, or forms of expression.

A Final Comment

When used as the basis for assessment, observations made of each of the nine processes provide qualitative data about the child that enables a teacher to judge the effectiveness of the musical program being offered. Teachers and other early childhood staff are accustomed to observing and recording children's behavior to inform curriculum development, implementation, and evaluation and typically select materials and learning experiences to accommodate each child's level of development and interest. However, observations of musical programs are typically undertaken less than in other curriculum areas, but they are equally important to understanding how children apply the musical processes to create personal meaning, to generate feedback to the children, and provide a basis for planning learning experiences. Observations must be specific and must focus on

a. the child's learning experience described through anecdotal information;
b. artistic elements that the child might use during the process;
c. the nine processes described above; and
d. planning implications.

   To synthesize the data, an observation sheet may be developed to reflect the grammar, syntax, sensory systems, and media of music's unique expression.

   To participate in arts education with this level of understanding, it is not sufficient for teachers of young children to be advocates for music; they must also have a deep knowledge of music and practice the processes of musicality. Unless the importance of literacy in music in early childhood is recognized, children may progress through school without having significant learning experiences. Furthermore, many children who may have the natural proclivity to excel in music may not have a chance to recognize their potential without adequate exposure to music and inspiration from educators who are responsive participants.

References

Alexander, R. R. (1982). Participant observation, ethnography, and their use in educational evaluation: A review of selected works. *Studies in Art Education, 24,* 63–69.

Almy, M., & Genishi, C. (1979). *Ways of studying children* (Rev. ed.). New York: Teachers College Press.

Alper, C. C. (1987). Early childhood music education. In C. Seefeldt (Ed.), *The early childhood curriculum: A review of current research* (pp. 237–250). New York: Teachers College Press.

Cole, E. S., & Schaefer, C. (1990). Can young children be art critics? *Young Children, 45,* 33–38.

Gardner, H. (1990, Dec.). *Assessment of student learning in the arts.* Paper presented at the Evaluating and Assessing the Visual Arts in Education Conference, Bosschenhoofdt, Netherlands.

McArdle, F., & Barker, B. (1990). *What'll I do for art today?* Melbourne: Nelson.

McLeod, J. (1990). *The arts and the year 2000.* Brisbane: Department of Education, Queensland.

Smith, N. (1980). Classroom practice: Creating meaning in the arts. In J. J. Hausman (Ed.), *Arts and the schools* (pp. 79–116). New York: McGraw-Hill.

Frances Rauscher is assistant professor of psychology at the University of Wisconsin-Oshkosh. This article originally appeared in the September 1998 issue of The Wisconsin School Musician. *Reprinted by permission.*

Assessing Musical Growth in Early Childhood

by Sister Lorna Zemke

At present, one of the most frequently discussed "buzz words" in education is "assessment." Recently, Silver Lake College spent more than a year "hammering out" a concerted assessment program for measuring student learning. The mission, goals and objectives of the institution were studied with a view toward a connection to an "Assessment Program for Student Academic Achievement."

Assessment can mean a multiplicity of things: formal types of evaluation such as standardized tests which carry numerical designations; charting a student's progress through observable, overt behavior; collecting bits and pieces of information as useful for stated specific purposes; self-assessment; peer assessment; and many shades and variations in between all of these.

What is valid assessment in an early childhood program? First and foremost, we as early childhood educators do need to be responsible for determining if each child is indeed growing musically and whether our instruction is effective. Simply put, do our children evidence overt behavior which indicates that musical learning is taking place?

General Assessment:

Some overall areas or goals which encompass all of early childhood music involves the children's ability to:

1. *imitate:* can children echo-perform a rhythmic or melodic pattern first initiated by the teacher?
2. *recognize:* can children identify a song when the teacher only hums or sings it on a neutral syllable?
3. *reproduce:* can children self-initiate singing a song or clapping the rhythm of a song "on their own" when given only the title of the song?

What are some observable musical behaviors/abilities in pre-schoolers and kindergartners which can be traced? A list might include: singing, sense of beat/rhythm, musical ear/listening ability, use of simple instruments, movement and games and improvisation, among others. Following are a few evaluative ideas:

Singing
Can the children…

- match pitches?
- sing in a group?
- sing alone?
- vocally flex and explore the voice?

Sense of Beat/Rhythm
Can the children…

- keep a steady beat?
- distinguish between beat and rhythm?
- echo clap rhythm patterns?
- sing faster/slower as directed?

Musical Ear/Listening Ability
Can the children…

- recognize songs when teacher hums them?
- recognize songs from pictures (visual representations)?
- recognize/demonstrate higher/lower?
- recognize/demonstrate louder/softer?
- recognize songs from opening phrases only?
- inner hear short rhymes/chants while "acting out" with appropriate motions?

Use of Simple Instruments
Can the children…

- keep a beat with instruments?
- move between beat and rhythm of a song?
- accompany a song or game?
- choose "correct" classroom instruments upon hearing their sound only?

Improvisation
Can the children…

- "make up" songs to story-telling?
- carry on "musical conversations"?
- create/think of new actions or ways to accompany a song?

Movement and Games
Can the children…

- use large muscle movements in musical play
- use small muscle movements (i.e., finger plays)
- move to music in "free play"
- participate in various singing gametypes (i.e., stationary circles, moving circles, partners, follow-the-leader, chase, etc.)

Two books may prove helpful if a teacher is searching for actual ways to format or chart their students' progress. They are *Music in Childhood: From Pre-school through the Elementary Grades* by Patricia Shehan-Campbell and Carol Scott-Kassner and *Musical Growth and Development (Birth Through Six)* by Dorothy T. McDonald and Gene M. Simons—both published by Schirmer.

The above presents a simple check-list to which teachers can add or subtract as seems appropriate. In the final analysis, the overriding "assessment" is the delight and joy which the children show by their eager and ready participation in the musical activities and experiences provided. Hopefully, these musical experiences sink deeply into the children's lives and make a difference for a lifetime.

Sister Lorna Zemke is professor of music education at Silver Lake College in Manitowoc, Wisconsin. This article originally appeared in the September 1998 issue of The Wisconsin School Musician. *Reprinted by permission.*

Other MENC Early Childhood Music Resources

Designing Music Environments for Early Childhood compiled by Susan H. Kenney and Diane Persellin. 2000. 54 pages. #1089.

Music in Prekindergarten: Planning and Teaching by Mary Palmer and Wendy L. Sims. 1993. 80 pages. #1031.

Opportunity-to-Learn Standards for Music Instruction: Grades PreK–12. 1994. 32 pages. #1619.

Performance Standards for Music: Strategies and Benchmarks for Assessing Progress Toward the National Standards, Grades PreK–12. 1996. 136 pages. #1633.

Prekindergarten Music Education Standards (brochure). 1995. #4015.

Promising Practices: Prekindergarten Music Education edited by Babara Andress. 1989. 120 pages. #1498.

Readings in Early Childhood Music Education edited and compiled by Barbara Andress and Linda Miller Walker. 1992. 112 pages. #1043.

The School Music Program—A New Vision: The K–12 National Standards, PreK Standards, and What They Mean to Music Educators. 1994. 48 pages. #1618.

Sing! Move! Listen! Music and Young Children (video). 1992. 18 minutes. #3081.

SoundPlay: Understanding Music through Creative Movement by Leon H. Burton and Takeo Kudo. 2000. 120 pages plus a 74-minute CD. #3003.

TIPS: Music Activities in Early Childhood compiled by John M. Feierabend. 1990. 32 pages. #1097.

For complete ordering information on these and other publications, contact:

MENC Publications Sales
1806 Robert Fulton Drive
Reston, VA 20191-4348

Credit card holders may call 1-800-828-0229.